Six Bullets at Sundown

A Novella by

Paul Grammatico

EJECT PRESS

To Nathan

PROLOGUE

IT WAS INDEPENDENCE DAY IN THE YEAR OF OUR LORD OF 1889, a warm early evening as the sun lowered in the south, shining brightly upon the town of Prosperity. It was situated in what folks would call the Wyoming territory in the Red Desert area. The town rose from its empty desert shell with its many large buildings that line the dusty, windswept main street. Once whitewashed, the buildings had a reddish haze due to the dusty soil that decorated this land. These wooden structures suffered many pockmarks due to the winds that carried the sand and the rocky impediments that had beaten up these buildings. When entering the town, all were greeted by Old Glory with its red and white stripes and blue field decorated with thirty-eight stars. Although worn and frayed at the edges from years of fierce wind and other elements, it flew on the flagpole and flapped defiantly in the breeze.

A celebration of freedom took place in the center of town. Patriotic red, white, and blue banners adorned each of the main street's saloons, hotels, storefronts, and the rectangular stage, which stood high above the crowd that gathered in front of it.

Several men stood on the stage, with many seated in wooden chairs at the back. One of the men, Jim Stanton, stepped up to the front. A man of average build and a bushy beard whose presence was unremarkable at best. He held up his hands for the crowd to quiet, as this was not just a day of independence for America.

"Today is the celebration of the one hundred and twenty-third year of our forefathers signing the Declaration of Independence," Jim declared loudly through his bushy beard as cheers rained down.

"Now, we'll have all the festivities in a minute," Jim's beard said, smiling and calming down the raucous crowd again. "I wanted to let you know that the election results are in, and we have our first mayor and sheriff!"

The crowd cheered and applauded with renewed and enhanced vigor. Jim looked past the frenzied crowd and saw, in the distance, a sizeable gang of men on horseback. Jim rubbed his eyes as if his sight deceived him. These men appeared out of thin air with no warning. The crowd's cheers brought Jim's eyes back to the audience.

"I want to introduce our new Sheriff, Tom Condon!" Jim declared. The crowd provided polite applause.

Jim walked from the stage, and Tom Condon, a short, skinny man in his mid-thirties, replaced him in the front. His presence was deemed insignificant in the town, and no one would notice or care if he disappeared at any moment. His plain features exuded zero power. As Jim returned to the chairs, a hand caught him, stopping him in his tracks.

Stan Masterton, a man in his mid-forties with never

an ear he didn't like to bend or a spirit he nary imbibed. His baggy-lidded, bloodshot eyes were obscured by his bushy white eyebrows and impressive white handlebar mustache. He spoke through a stained, rotting fence of teeth.

"Tom's our sheriff? What kind of joke are you playing on me, Jim?" Stan angrily hissed.

"We couldn't get anyone else to take the job. He's all we got."

Stan's hand dropped from Jim's arm; his face formed a mask of contempt and disgust.

Tom removed his hat and bowed as if praying to someone or anyone. He felt like a fool that anyone would convince him to be a lawman. He had no idea what the right and wrong sides of the law were. He was as surprised as anyone when he became elected to this post. *Might as well git this over with*, Tom thought as he shuffled toward the front of the stage. A breeze blew through Tom's brown, shaggy hair, entangling it in various waves and forms. Tom raised his eyes, looked down at the decent-sized crowd, and wished he could disappear into the air.

"Well, I ain't so good at makin' speeches, so I just want to thank y'all who voted for me, and I'll do my best to make you proud," Tom mumbled to the crowd who clapped half-heartedly, knowing they were doomed.

Jim stepped in front of Tom and guided him away from the front of the stage. Tom shuffled away to the back of the stage with Stan, whose contemptible face remained, shaking his head in anger mixed with worry.

"Thanks, Tom. Now, I would like to introduce our first mayor. A man that needs no introduction, Stan Masterton."

As the crowd roared and clapped loudly, the gang on horseback slowly approached. Jim turned his back on the crowd and tried to get Stan's attention by pointing at the horde in the distance. Stan got up from his chair, grabbed Jim gently by the shoulders, and moved him out of the way when he moved to the center of the stage. His head held high with confidence bordering on arrogance that oozed out of his being.

"As Tom rightly said, he's not good at making speeches, but I don't have that problem."

The crowd erupted into laughter and cheered as Stan returned their racket with a sly grin and a wink.

"Especially if I've had a few too many over at Jim's Saloon," Stan needled as he pointed at Jim, making the audience laugh even louder. Stan waved his arms with his palms facing down—a signal for calm as Stan's face fell into a tight, stern replica of a fist.

"This is a momentous time for Prosperity, aptly named for the beautiful landscapes and wildlife. But what is more important than any of that, Prosperity's greatest natural resource is its people."

A roar of acceptance emerged from the crowd. Stan looked upon the outskirts of the town, where the gang of men moved closer and closer. He cleared his throat nervously and continued.

"As Wyoming territory is on the verge of statehood, we must be the example of what a good, strong Wyoming town should be. A foundation of law and order!" Stan bellowed loudly, hoping to scare off the distant clan, but the result was futile as the roars from the crowd doubled, and they advanced right to the edge of the town.

"As our Founding Fathers gained our independence, we in Prosperity must do—"

Suddenly, the intruders charged into the town. Stan, Tom, and Jim pulled their guns from their holsters, along with the other men on the stage.

The crowd heard the loud, vibrating rumble of hooves and saw the men pulling their guns. The crowd scattered in all directions to escape the gang and the men onstage. Some of the gang headed for the stage.

The men on the stage fired their guns, with the marauders returning fire. Their bullets hit the men on the stage. They fell onto the wooden planks—stone dead. Some of the women and men from the crowd attempted to run away. The bloody men roared with laughter as they shot at the crowd.

Other townsfolk pulled their guns and returned fire. The crew cut them down. The main street was in sheer chaos. Gunfire hailed in all directions, with bystanders and crowd members feeling the wrath of the bullets. The invaders grabbed women in the street.

All the hell in the world had broken loose.

ONE

STRANGER ON HORSEBACK TROTTED INTO PROSPERITY. His long hair and vast flowing beard had taken over his head and face. What little skin was seen upon his face looked weather-beaten from all his days riding in the desert.

The man was an alien to this town. His thin, wiry body was covered in a costume, giving him a circus sideshow flair that had seen far better days. His horse was on the older side but still had tremendous musculature.

The stranger surveyed the town. He had been here before and knew this town too well. Many ghosts haunted each town he traveled to, but the specters here were intense— a product of the past. Black dots spotted the town, courtesy of an extreme amount of bullets violating the many sides of each building. Old Glory fluttered in the breeze. Its fabric bored more holes in its stars and stripes and clung desperately to the pole. The stranger knew this emblem would escape and dance with the wind. Faded figures advancing upon the town crept into his mind—the past phantoms had returned.

"Howdy."

The amicable voice snapped the man out of his observations and ghostly reveries. He spied on an elderly man, Cyrus Johnson. He was a short, heavyset man of sixty years, cleaned around his building that said, 'Cyrus' General Store.' The man pulled the reins, and the horse stopped. He would feign ignorance—he had to.

"Hello," the newcomer replied.

"Can I help you?"

"I suppose. I've been to this town, but I can't remember. It was some time ago. It's on the tip of my tongue. Pre… pro—"

"Prosperity."

"Prosperity," he quickly said with a snap of his fingers. "I remember." The stranger looked around the town, seeing the mayhem that had transpired days ago. "Hmmm… what the hell happened here? Looks like you got a prosperity of bullets all over this town."

"You could say that," Cyrus stiffly replied.

"You got a mayor in this town? A sheriff?"

"We voted for 'em, but…"

As if the interloper was psychic or a victim of perfect timing, the sound of clopping resounded through the main street, and a horse-drawn wagon came into view with a well-dressed, ancient man who looked damn near a hundred years old pulled at the reins. Two wooden plank coffins were in plain sight as the wagon rolled out of town.

"You're lookin' at 'em," Cyrus said. His tone was as dry as the sand swirling in the town. "What's left of 'em, anyway."

"I see," the fellow flatly stated.

"Name's Cyrus, by the way. Got a name, stranger?"

"Stranger," the man mused, "I like it. You can call me that."

"Really?"

"Yep."

An uncomfortable silence followed. Cyrus looked up and down at the Stranger's odd choice of clothing. *Ain't no getup I've ever seen around these parts*, thought Cyrus. He'd seen pictures of similar outfits drawn out on some postcards, but Cyrus hadn't seen anything like this in the flesh.

"Mister, are you lost? Did you get separated from your Wild West show or somethin'?"

"No, no… nothing like that," he replied with a soft chuckle. "It looks pretty bad, don't it? Got this at some trading post. All they had that fit."

"I got some clothes at my store if you have some money. I'm sure I got somethin' that'll fit."

"Mighty kind of ya, but they'll do for now. I'm lookin' for some people, and I think they've been around these parts."

"Who ya lookin' for?" Cyrus asked.

"The Jackson Gang," the Stranger replied. "Mainly Jericho Jackson."

"The Jackson Gang? What in hell do ya want them fer?"

"Well, they owe me something, and I mean to get it back."

"They gave us something all right," Cyrus replied, indicating the torn-up town.

"I see that."

"How can ya not?" Cyrus exclaimed. "I'm afraid they'd do the same number on you."

"I aim to get what I came for," said the Stranger.

"I would turn you and your horse right out of this town," snapped Cyrus.

"Nope, got a job to do," the Stranger replied.

"And how do you gonna do that? Got a posse?"

"Just me."

Cyrus looked at this odd man and was not impressed. He shook his head. *This insane fool's gonna get killed.*

"They're a gang," Cyrus explained. He felt like he was talking to a precocious child.

"I know that," the Stranger coolly replied.

"Where's your guns?"

He put his hand on his gun—a stunning 1872 Colt Single Action with a dark rosewood handle.

"Right here," said the man, gently patting the firearm as one would playfully do to a child.

"That six-shooter? That's all ya got?"

"All I ever use."

"Listen Stranger, they got all sorts of guns and ammo. They'll put more holes in you than they did this town."

"Yeah… impressive."

"You'll be gettin' yourself in a heap of trouble, and you ain't gonna get much help here. They took care of that."

"I'm pretty sure it will all work out just fine," the cocksure Stranger said.

"For them or you?"

A smile formed on the Stranger's face. Incredulous at the man's reaction, Cyrus shook his head. *I can't believe he's gonna go through with it! This can't be real!*

"You are plum loco."

"Well, this loco needs a drink." The Stranger broadly grinned.

"Jim's Saloon's down there a ways," Cyrus informed him.

"Care to join me?"

"Why not? Not gettin' much, if any, business today."

Cyrus locked the store and walked with the stranger with his horse that trotted down the dusty red street, passing each hotel and storefront. *This might be the last time I see this poor feller,* Cyrus thought, as an edge of sadness crossed his face. *He'll be out in that cemetery like so many others.*

"Never witnessed a man's last drink before," Cyrus stated.

"Ye of little faith," He replied with a wink.

"Preacher, are ya? Givin' me some god talk or somethin' like that, huh? You need to tell god to come and give us a hand."

"How do ya mean?"

"We're workin' on statehood."

"Statehood?"

"Yeah, you're in Wyoming territory."

"Really?"

"Yeah. We're tryin' to be a civilized community. We don't need someone to be takin' other people's lives."

"I see."

"We need some kinda structure. With laws and a court to enforce them. That hands down penalties and repentance."

"And to penalize with death if needed?"

"Well... yeah."

"Hmmm… that's civilized, I reckon."

The Stranger and Cyrus got to Jim's Saloon, an unremarkable place with a faded red-painted wood sign and cracked slats of swinging doors that moved back and forth to the rhythm of the gentle breeze.

"Well, this here's the place."

The man looked around the hitching post, but the horizontal wooden posts were filled with horses. Surprise and confusion crossed the man's face until Cyrus gently tapped him on the leg and pointed across the street.

"There's a hitching post that's empty over there. I'll wait for ya."

The Stranger nodded, dismounted, guided his horse across the street, and tied the reins to one of the posts. He returned to Cyrus and entered Jim's Saloon.

The saloon had small, round tables with chairs strewn about the central area of the bar, with men playing cards and women behind some of them or joining in on the card games. When they passed by, some men and women suppressed their laughs at his weird dress.

Despite being in a desert environment with sand and dust covering the floor, the saloon gave off a musty smell. A combination of sweat and tobacco smoke emanating from cheap cigars and rolled cigarettes permeated the room. The log cabin walls and the bar swelled and bulged from the moisture of human sweat and smoke. The Stranger and Cyrus approached the bar and met up with Jessy, who was tending it. Aged in her middle thirties, but living in the desert had wrinkled her, carving her into a hardened beauty. She served drinks to the men at the bar. The men leered at her, but she ignored them as she approached Cyrus and the newcomer.

The Stranger gazed at Jessy. Age had eliminated the innocence he once saw many years ago, but in his eyes, her beauty remained.

"What'll you boys have?" Jessy sighed in exhaustion.

"Bourbon if ya got it," replied Cyrus.

She nodded at Cyrus, turned to the unknown man, and looked at his outfit—a slight smile creased upon her hardened face.

"What about you, Carnival Man?" Jessy mused.

The men at the bar chuckled when they placed the foppish intruder in their view.

"Same," the Stranger flatly replied.

She poured each bourbon into a shot glass and served them at the bar.

"You tendin' this evening?" Cyrus inquired.

"Ain't it obvious?

A flare of contempt ensued between Cyrus and Jessy as Jessy turned to this odd fellow, looking at his outrageous outfit. Her musing turned to pity as she felt sorry for this strange man. She peered into his eyes. The shades of hazel gave her a sense of familiarity. She had seen these eyes before but couldn't place them in her mind.

"Didn't mean nothin' by the crack I gave ya," Jessy said.

"None taken. Heard far worse," the Stranger replied.

"So, what's with your get-up? You get lost from your troupe?"

"That's what I said to him," Cyrus said, cutting into her conversation.

"Nah. I'm looking for some people."

"He wants the Jackson gang," Cyrus interrupted.

The men at the bar stopped their activity and stared straight at the Stranger, disbelief and scorn etched upon their faces. The Stranger stared back at the men with an uncaring smile. A long silence filled the saloon as all the patrons stopped what they were doing and stared at the intruder as if they viewed a plague upon him. Jessy furiously shook her head, refusing to believe what she heard. The message was received—loud and clear.

"Oh, you want nothin' to do with them."

Outside, the familiar clopping sound of the hooves of the two horses pulling the same cart with a coffin and the same ancient man at the reins guiding the horses out-of-town past the saloon door.

"Why don't you ask him? Or what's left of him."

"Jim of this saloon?"

"Yep... the gang you wanna go after made mincemeat outta him."

"Yeah, I saw a few more coffins goin' out to the cemetery. Why so many corpses? And this town bein' so shot up?"

"We tried to make a break from the Jackson gang. Especially Jericho Jackson," Jessy replied with gloom. "We thought we could make this town normal and safe instead of insane and lawless."

"Yeah, Cyrus told me you wanted statehood or somethin'."

"Jericho must've caught wind about what we were doin' and brought his outlaws to crush us and our chances."

"I don't know about all that. All I know is they got

something of mine that I want."

"And you think you're gonna get it from them?" Jessy said.

"I expect to," the Stranger replied.

"And it's just you?"

"Just me."

"You're outta your damn mind," Jessy grumbled.

"Yeah, I've been told that," the Stranger replied.

"They told you right. Leave… there's nothin' for you here."

"I ain't going nowhere until I get what I came for."

Suddenly, the bar vibrated. The intensity increased with the rising clamor of hoofbeats as the uproar rumbled toward the saloon, kicking up dust through the swinging doors.

"Lookin' like you're gonna get your chance," Jessy replied.

The hoofbeats stopped. Voices and gunshots were heard. Everybody in the bar turned to the swinging doors. The stranger didn't look back and drank his drink. A horde of six men entered into the saloon. These men were part of the Jackson gang. Everybody quickly returned to what they were doing before the gang arrived. The group of six went up to the bar. A broad-shouldered, stout man whose age looked to be in his early thirties, with pockmarks and scars decorating his overly large Cro-Magnon face, slammed his hand on the bar and glowered at Jessy.

"Whisky! Bottle!"

Jessy placed the bottle on the bar along with some shot glasses.

"Yeah, won't be needin' those."

Jessy, her face twisted in disgust, put the glasses back behind the bar. The gang member looked at the unusual intruder up and down.

"Well, who in hell we got here?"

Another gang member came over; the slim, rat-faced young man broke into a grin.

"Look at the fancy man."

Another member came around, a tall, handsome man with pitch-black hair slicked back. He looked like some dandy, wearing brightly colored clothes that would blind most humans.

"Hell, I didn't know the circus was in town."

Another gang member completed the circle around the Stranger with the other three. Tall but very wiry, dressed all in black with a wide mustache. He strode over, solid and confident—the alpha amongst these deltas.

"You get lost from the rest of your freaks?" The leader said.

"Why no, Alonzo," the Stranger pleasantly replied. "I didn't get lost."

"How- how'n hell do you know my name?" Alonzo said.

"Why, hell, I know all of ya," the Stranger said. "That's your brother Bart, Boone, Cassidy, Bill, and Carson."

"How do you know our names?" Alonzo pressed.

"Aren't you all part of the Jackson Gang?"

"And how do you know that?" Alonzo pressed again.

"You're known all over this territory. There are posters everywhere with your names and faces on 'em."

The Stranger looked at the slick-haired dandy. He

was the kind of man looking for anything in which to see his reflection. If vanity killed, he would be stone dead.

"Carson Cloutier. Cattle rustling, assault with a deadly weapon, attempted murder, but you ain't considered dangerous."

He turned to the older rat-faced man, the exact opposite of Carson, who looked worse upon each viewing and would crack and dent anything that mirrored his image.

"Bill Tenney. Fraud, cheating at cards, bribery, horse theft. Oh, and selling guns to the Natives with some murder in there somewhere."

The Stranger looked over to a red-haired man whose frame looked more like a bare-knuckled brawler than a shootist. The scars that lined his face and his swollen hands indicated that he had lost many more fights than he had won.

"Cassidy O'Brien. Horse theft, arson, attempted murder, assault with a deadly weapon, and… drunkenness."

He looked around to see a short, broad-chested man with long brown sideburns. His grizzled features and large hands made him look more bear than man; the Stranger shook his head.

"Boone Johnson. More of the same as the others."

The Stranger then glared right into the tall, wide-mustached man. His slim frame, long arms, thin fingers, and long, thin nose made his features look like an oversized albatross, which would have made the captain in Coleridge's *Rime of the Ancient Mariner* shrink in horror if he had to hang this man around his neck.

"Alonzo Clanton. Horse theft, murder, cattle rustling, selling whisky to natives, bank and train robberies. You're considered very dangerous, but your brother, now that's a different story."

He focused on the scarred, pockmarked face pasted upon his elongated skull, accentuated by the man's balding head. His flat face, resulting from far too many bar brawls and other mayhem, made him a mouth breather, displaying his crooked, brown, tobacco-stained teeth with each inhale.

"Bart… now you're a bad one. Murders, horse thefts, cheating at cards, robberies, assaults, rustling… I could go on and on, but I think you and everyone here get the idea. You are a very, very dangerous man."

The fop lifted his glass of bourbon from the bar and saluted to no one in particular.

"Reward! Dead or Alive!" the stranger declared as he downed his bourbon and slammed the shot glass on the bar. The hushed saloon attendees looked on in horror.

"Ain't nobody gonna take any of us alive or dead," rumbled Alonzo.

"I see," the Stranger replied.

"You see and say a bit too much for my likin'," Bart growled.

"Maybe we should make you dead," Bill sneered.

"Sounds good to me," Carson replied.

The gang descended on the Stranger and grabbed him from all sides. He stood at the bar despite the gang rooting him up from his spot.

A rifle barrel jutted out from the bar and pointed at the lawbreakers. The criminals backed away from the Stranger. At the other end of the rifle — Jessy.

"You ain't doing any of that horseshit inside this bar,"

Jessy firmly stated.

"We weren't going to do anything to 'em," Carson said sheepishly, taking his hands off the drifter.

"Yeah, we were gonna have a little talk, that's all." Alonzo softened his grip and patted the man gently.

"And you expect me to believe that?" Jessy replied, still pointing the rifle.

"Little girls shouldn't be playin' with guns. Someone might get hurt," Bart snarled.

"I'm not seeing any girls in here, and I'll take my chances because I'm not playing with ya," Jessy hissed.

"Easy with that," Bill said with his hands up.

"You've already shot up the town. I'll be damned if you're gonna shoot up my bar," Jessy replied, her anger rising.

"Your bar? Says who?" Carson asked.

"You killed Jim, so I guess I gotta take over."

"Wasn't us. We had nothin' to do with that," Bill replied.

"Bill the bullshitter. You know that's what they call you around here, right?"

"Look, we don't want to kill a woman. We're gentlemen," Alonzo said.

"You can stop all that silver-tongued chivalry shit. You take it outside, or some of you can join Jim in the cemetery outside town!" Jessy barked.

"We could kill you so easily!" Bart thundered.

"I'll take that chance." Jessy sneered as she cocked her rifle, "So, who's first?"

"Whoa, whoa…we don't need to have any of that

here!" Alonzo exclaimed as he advanced to the back of the Stranger, who never turned his head to look at him. "Tell you what we'll do. We'll give you until sundown to leave town. Sound fair?"

The Stranger remained silent as he motioned for Jessy to fill up his glass again, to which Jessy responded with a glower of hot anger, still holding her rifle at the ready.

"Let's go," Alonzo told the rest of his men, and the gang headed toward the exit. Alonzo turned back to the Stranger's neck.

"Remember… sundown."

Alonzo grabbed the bottle from the bar, and the gang left the saloon single-file through the swinging doors.

Jessy lowered the rifle with shaking hands and breathed a massive sigh of relief. She turned and glared at the Stranger, who sat like a stoic stone effigy.

"I'd do what he says… "

TWO

THE GANG LEFT THE SALOON, WENT TO THE HITCHING POSTS IN front, and untied their horses' reins. The felons got ready to mount their horses, hoping not to return and finish some business at sundown. This meddlesome Stranger would prove otherwise and bring them back. Alonzo cursed under his breath at this inevitable scenario.

Bart was about to mount his horse when he spied the Stranger's horse across the main street. Adorned with the same accouterments as the odd man's outfit, his face broke into a misshapen grin as he observed the horse and its strange attire.

"Well, look at fancy man's horse," Bart laughed and walked across the main street.

"Bart, where are you going?" Alonzo asked.

"I just wanna see his horse, that's all!" Bart replied.

He crossed over to the adjacent hitching and arrived to the right side of the mysterious man's horse. He examined the horse from the tip of its nose to the end of its tail.

"Look at this old nag!" Bart exclaimed. "Ain't you pretty!"

Bart struck the horse straight in the ribs with his fist. The horse buckled from the blow but managed to keep itself upright. The horse huffed to recover from the assault on its torso.

"Pretty old!" Bart guffawed.

"C'mon Bart! We don't have time for this!" Alonzo shouted.

"But I do…'sides, I'm just havin' a little fun with his horse," Bart replied. He patted the horse on the back of its neck. "Ain't that right?"

Bart walked to the front of the horse and tried to grab its reins. The horse dodged his hand by shaking its head from side to side, out of Bart's reach. Bart continued to reach and grab for the black leather strips, his hand coming up empty on each attempt.

"C'mere, you son of a bitch," Bart growled.

Bart extended his hand further to grab the horse's bridle. The horse turned its head, opened its mouth, and clamped down hard on Bart's right forearm. Bart yelped loudly and struggled to free his arm from the horse's mouth, but the horse had his arm and held it fast between its jaws. Bart's face dissolved from hate to panic. He pulled harder at his arm. The horse sank its teeth further into Bart's flesh. Bart huffed and whined with desperate attempts to rescue his arm and cease the pain that throbbed endlessly. The gang moved toward Bart and the horse, unsure of what they had witnessed.

CRACK!

Bart let out a cry that was loud enough for Alonzo and his crew to hear but couldn't penetrate the din of the saloon. The horse crunched into the bone in Bart's forearm. It snapped and then twisted his arm at an odd and sickening angle as Bart gritted and hissed through his teeth in agony.

The gang viewed this atrocity and stopped cold in the middle of the street. The horse sunk its teeth further and shook its head. Something dropped into the sand. The horse severed Bart's arm clean from his body! The blood spurted and streamed down the useless stump of his arm; the metallic odor of vital fluid, which was his friend from the victims he'd once savaged, became his mortal enemy. He held the bloody stump with his good hand in a futile effort to stop the bleeding. He stumbled backward to the horse's rump—it was some form of fate or karma. The horse raised its back legs and kicked Bart square in the head, killing him. The impact of the kick on Bart's body sprayed blood and gore upon the entire gang, especially Alonzo, who was in front of the clan. He touched his face and pulled his hand away. It revealed the gory remains of his brother. He walked back into the bar with the gang following. He headed straight for the Stranger.

"Your goddamn horse killed my brother!"

"A man should know better than to mess with another man's animal," the Stranger replied stone-faced. He took his drink off the bar and finished it in one gulp.

"Forget about sundown. We're gonna take care of you right now!"

Alonzo and the gang grabbed the Stranger from the bar, dragged him out of the saloon, and pushed him through the swinging doors and into the windblown, dust-filled outdoors.

Alonzo grabbed the Stranger's gun out of his holster. The gang pushed the unknown man with the murderous horse into the center of the street. Everyone in the saloon, along with several store owners, gathered along the sides of the street.

Jessy pushed her way to get a front-row view at the clash of the gun-toting gladiators, which, if she was a bettor, would go down as well as a one-legged man in an ass-kicking contest.

The Stranger reached for his gun, which wasn't there — not a good look so far. The gang drew out their guns as he smiled sheepishly and raised his arms to the sky in feigned surrender.

"You plan on shooting an unarmed man? Don't seem fair to me."

Alonzo emptied the bullets from the chambers of the six-shooter, took one bullet, put it in the chamber, slammed the cylinder shut, and threw the gun in the sand next to him.

"There's your fair," Alonzo replied with a smirk.

The Stranger went for his gun. The gang opened fire on him. The man dove away from the gunfire and picked up the gun. He shot at Cassidy. The bullet went through Cassidy's forehead, exiting out the back of his head. The Stranger transferred the gun to his left hand. He flicked his right wrist and, out of his sleeve, emerged a cylinder packed with six bullets, which landed in his hand.

With a quick flip of his hand, the cylinder exited his hand and whirled into the air. He lined up his gun, pulled a switch that ejected the used-up cylinder, and guided the new cylinder into the gun. The spun cylinder lined up perfectly into the space where the old cylinder used to be.

The new cylinder clicked into the gun. The Stranger

shot and killed Bill, Carson, and Boone with three shots in lightning succession. The gang members were gunned down with various killing shots to their chest, neck, and head. The Stranger shot Alonzo in the hand. Alonzo squealed in pain and dropped his gun.

As Alonzo tried to reclaim the gun. He shot the gun away from him with his last two bullets. Alonzo was unsure what to do next. The crowd had witnessed this showdown in silence. Jessy jostled to keep her place in the front and gaped in amazement. She measured up the odd man who came uninvited into her town. An epiphany of recognition flashed into her skull.

"Johnny… Johnny One…"

Alonzo held his bleeding hand. Johnny shifted the gun into his right hand, pointed his gun at Alonzo, and pulled the trigger again and again, The gun's hammer clicking away. Johnny was out of ammo. He ejected the cylinder out of his gun and snapped his left wrist. A fresh cylinder loaded with bullets fell into his hand. He shoved the cylinder into the gun.

"Go tell your boss Jerry to come and see me," said Johnny.

Alonzo grabbed his gun, ran toward his horse, mounted it, and rode out of town. The crowd clapped and cheered. Johnny put his gun back into his holster. Men, women, and children approached Johnny, shook his hand, embraced, and grabbed at him.

"Mister, how did you do that?" Cyrus cried.

"Oh, that? Aw, just some trick I learned along the way," Johnny humbly replied.

"But you lied to me, Mister."

"I didn't lie. I told you I had one gun. I never said I had six bullets."

"I have to say, that's the best shootin' I ever saw!" Cyrus declared.

"It was nothin'," Johnny replied. He turned to the crowd. "It's all fine now. You can all go back to what you were doin'."

Johnny pulled himself away from the crowd and back into the saloon. The crowd followed along. Johnny went to the bar with Jessy behind it.

"All right!" Jessy barked. "If nobody's going to be drinkin' here, you need to clear out right now! I know you all had a lot to do in this town before all this happened, so go on!"

"You should re-open your store. With all the excitement, you might get a customer or two," Johnny said.

"You're right. I'll see ya later," Cyrus replied. He quickly exited the saloon.

Jessy filled Johnny's glass and inspected him like she was seeing an old friend. It was ages and spaces between them for so long that they knew full well that they weren't the same people — physically or mentally. They were unknown to each other. She nodded tentatively and stared through Johnny's thick, gnarled black beard.

"I finally figured out who you are," Jessy said.

"Did you?" Johnny replied.

"Johnny One."

"I'm impressed. What finally gave me away?"

"The eyes... and that trick you pulled."

"I was afraid of that."

"I've seen that trick before."

"In my act?"

"Only I've never seen you do it that fast before."

"I just got better," Johnny quipped.

"And older," Jessy replied.

Jessy grabbed the lapel of his leather coat. She jerked back in disgust at the acrid smell. She had witnessed the stench of dead animals, but this was worse than anything her nostrils had encountered. Her nostrils never stung when she first met Johnny.

"Along with your clothes. Let's get ya cleaned up."

She motioned to another bartender, a rail-thin man with red hair and a long mustache on the other side of the bar. The ginger came over and let her know he was at her service.

"Hey Wesley, can you take over for me?"

The redhead nodded in acknowledgment. Johnny and Jessy made their way up the stairs, hoping she could find out what happened to Johnny and if he was a shade of the man she once knew or if time and experiences made him a nameless shadow — taking on a deadly horde of men who would seal his demise.

THREE

JESSY KNOCKED ON THE DOOR AND OPENED IT. JOHNNY WAS sitting naked in a bathtub filled with suds that spilled over the edge. He had the kerchief tied around his neck. Jessy entered the room with a bundle of clothes. The room's long French doors jutted onto an expansive wooden balcony. The sun's glow setting in the distance.

"Went over to Cyrus' store. He gave me these. Thought they would fit ya," Jessy stated.

"Much obliged," Johnny amicably replied.

"It's nearly sundown. Looks like you're stickin' around?" Jessy asked.

"Lookin' that way," Johnny replied.

Jessy put the new pile of clothes on her chair next to her flowery, hand-carved, darkened mahogany mirrored vanity table, courtesy of Cyrus a master with a knife and a block of wood.

"All he had was black," Jessy said. "No one wears much dark clothin' in these parts."

"Black's fine by me," Johnny replied.

Jessy grabbed his old clothes, and the acrid smell returned to her olfactory senses. *Damn! This had to be the worst smell I've ever had to deal with in my life!*

"I should put these in a pit and set fire to 'em," said Jessy.

Jessy dropped the odorous clothing in the far corner of the room. She went to the vanity, grabbed scissors, and approached Johnny. She eyed the enormous black mess that resided on top of his head and the black mass growing out of his face. Jessy knew she had some work to do.

"What are those for?" Johnny asked.

"I'm gonna fix you up," Jessy gently replied. "Lean back."

Johnny leaned back in the tub. Jessy grabbed the kerchief hung around his neck and gently shook it. She knew something horrible had happened to Johnny, but she wasn't sure what. Her mind had an idea, but it would never be confirmed unless he told her, which might be an exercise in futility.

"Why do you still have this thing on?" Jessy said. She regretted the words that emerged from her mouth.

"I have my reasons," Johnny replied.

"Suit yourself."

"You normally cut men's hair?" said Johnny.

"Used to cut Jim's," replied Jessy.

"Damn... sorry about that," Johnny said.

"It's okay. You get used to death in these parts," Jessy replied.

Jessy took water from the tub and wet the back of his hair. She took a bar of soap and massaged the suds into his scalp.

"I remember seeing your show around these parts

when I was a young girl."

"I remember."

After a few moments of massage, Jessy removed her hands, doused Johnny's hair with water, and dried his gigantic mound of black hair. Taking the scissors, she held down a piece of his hair from the back and snipped it off.

"Never saw anything like it before," she stated.

Jessy turned the scissors and snipped another piece of Johnny's hair. She kept trimming away. The rhythm of the clipping transported her mind to when Prosperity was a different town—a different time.

§

A large axe flew through the air and landed on a wood log with a hard *thunk*. A target is painted on the face of the log. The axe landed straight into the center—a perfect bullseye. Two Native American twins in their forties, Herrick and Olowin, were revealed. They were burly, muscular men dressed in traditional dress and face paint. One of the men threw another axe towards the target. He split the head of the axe handle of the embedded axe right down the center—a perfect throw. The crowd of Prosperity gasped and cheered at the skill and accuracy of the men. The sideshow barker, Archer McCoy, came to the area next to the men. He was foppishly dressed in a large top hat and carried a cane in his right hand. Holding a megaphone in his left hand, he placed it to his mouth, which was lined with a long, white goatee.

"Let's give a round of applause to the axe-throwing twins, Herrick and Olowin!"

Herrick and Olowin turned toward the crowd and smiled. The crowd applauded in appreciation of their remarkable skill. Herrick and Olowin bowed to the crowd. In front of the crowd who enthusiastically joined the throng stood a younger version of Jessy, about eighteen. Awkward and gangly, but potential for her beauty to blossom — an innocent girl in the early flower of her womanhood.

"Now, for our next act, we have a man from parts unknown who has drawn and beaten some of the greatest gunfighters and gangs all along this territory. And the wondrous part of defeating all of these bandits and outlaws, ladies and gentlemen, is that he only does it with one gun! One gun gets it done! So, without further ado, I give you the greatest man ever to hold a hog leg. The one, the only, Johnny One!"

A younger Johnny in his early twenties came out to the crowd. Clad head to toe in a fancy, light-tanned, leathery outfit similar to what Johnny blew into town with. His large, pecan-colored cowboy hat and black kerchief, which covered his face, made him an intimidating figure.

The crowd backed away. He pulled the brim of his hat back and removed the kerchief from his face. He flung the kerchief dramatically, revealing a young, boyish face with tattoos on his cheeks and the upper and lower parts of his mouth. On his left cheek, he had a black club, a red diamond on his right cheek, a red heart on his lower lip, and a black spade between his nose and upper lip. The crowd gasped and cheered.

Johnny took a silver dollar from his pocket and tossed it. He pulled out his gun and shot one time into the air. He caught the silver dollar as it came back down to earth. He showed it to the crowd. — a perfect hole in the center of the silver dollar. The crowd cheered once more. A smiling and amicable Johnny strolled over to the crowd.

"I need a volunteer. Would someone like to assist me?" Johnny said.

Jessy stepped out of the crowd. *Damn, he is so handsome,* Jessy thought. Johnny saw Jessy, and a broad smile crossed his face, filling up his prominent cheeks as they dimpled.

Johnny took Jessy's hand. When Johnny's dry, rough skin touched her soft, long fingers, Jessy was surprised at the sensation but didn't find it unpleasant.

"Well, howdy there. What's your name?" Johnny said.

"Jessy, sir," she croaked.

"Well, you don't have to call me all that. I'm just Johnny. Treat me as… a friend."

"Yes, sir."

The crowd laughed at the routine. Jessy's face flushed in embarrassment at the unintended comedy routine. She raised her head and met Johnny's. His face never broke its wonderful smile. It calmed her.

"C'mon Jessy. We're gonna have some fun!"

Johnny guided Jessy into the shooting area. The crowd applauded. Johnny gave her a deck of playing cards and whispered instructions in her ear. She walked away from Johnny, stopped, and turned. Johnny made a circular motion around his face to Jessy. Jessy nodded in the affirmative, flipped over the deck of cards, and spread them out in her hands.

Johnny flipped the gun to his left hand and covered up the heart tattoo on his lower lip. Jessy took the four hearts out of the deck and threw the card into the air. Johnny aimed the gun in his left hand and shot four bullets. The card came tumbling down to the ground. Jessy picked up the card and showed it to the crowd. Within the four hearts on the cards were four bullet holes placed squarely in the center of each heart. The crowd gasped and applauded.

Jessy returned to where she had initially stood. She met Johnny's eyes. She took the deck of cards, placed them in her left hand, and fanned herself with them. Laced with cat-calls and guffaws of delight over Jessy's improvisation.

Damn, she's a natural, thought Johnny. *I could take her on the road and create our own act.*

Jessy stopped fanning herself. Johnny switched the gun to his right hand. He covered the club and the diamond tattoos on his face with his left hand. Jessy threw up two cards. Johnny used his last shot in the chamber, flicked out a cylin-der from his left sleeve, ejected the empty cylinder from the gun, shoved a full cylinder in its place, and fired at the cards.

He covered the heart and the spade tattoo, and Jessy threw up two more cards. Johnny fired, switching with each hand, and flicked out cylinders from each sleeve, coming in hot. He covered up three of his tattoos; three cards went up while he fired and reloaded. He covered up all four tattoos for his final act, and four cards went up.

When the gun smoke cleared, empty bullet casings and cylinders were strewn about Johnny's feet. All around Jessy was the entire deck of cards. Once thrown in the air, now lay in the sand.

Jessy looked at the cards where bullet holes resided. She gestured to the crowd to see the cards up close. The crowd walked around and looked at the various cards. The crowd passed by and left the cards in the sand. They moved on to the next attraction as Archer guided them along. The crowd got smaller and faded away in the distance. Pairs of boots stepped on the cards — a menacing pack of death.

§

Jessy kept cutting with her scissors while Johnny remained in the tub. She managed to unsnarl the mop of hair. It made Johnny a man and not a wild beast clad in clownish clothes.

"Not bad, but that beard…" Jessy whispered as she went towards the beard with her scissors. Johnny jolted back as if the scissors were a branding iron.

"Easy with those."

"I just want to trim it a little bit, that's all," Jessy said.

"All right now, but not too much," Johnny replied.

"Why are you hiding?" sighed Jessy. She started trimming his beard.

"I think you know why, considering how many friends I made today," replied Johnny.

Jessy kept snipping away. *Well, I'm right about one thing: he's not the boyish young man I once knew, but then again, I'm not the gangly, awkward girl I was either! Don't know who he's hiding from, but he is still a damn fine man despite all of the hair!*

"Did you shoot through all of those cards way back when?" Jessy asked.

"A man once told me that a good magician doesn't give away nothin'."

"That's no answer."

"Did you believe that I did?"

"I… I did."

"Well then, a belief is better than any reality."

"What man told you that?"

"The one whose hair you're cuttin'."

"I know how you shot through those cards."

"I believe you were sworn to secrecy when you volunteered."

"Was I?"

"Yep," said Johnny.

"All I know is I'll never forget that day."

As Jessy's rhythmic snipping continued, it created a hypnotic state. In his mind, he was transported back twelve years to a day he'd like to forget.

§

The boots remained standing on the cards in the sand. The boots were attached to a gang of men. The gang made their walk towards the faraway crowd.

§

Johnny snapped out of his spell. He saw himself in a mirror held by Jessy. He hadn't had any grooming for some time. There were too many towns with too many people who were good, bad, and everything in between. He didn't bother to look into mirrors. Thus, he never knew what he looked like until now. He didn't look too bad on the outside, but there was the inside…

"What do you think? Not bad, eh?" Jessy boasted.

"Not bad," Johnny replied. He examined her work. *I can't say when's the last time someone did a job on this head of hair… and a damn fine one at that!* Johnny thought.

Jessy went to her vanity, put down the scissors, and started taking off her clothes.

"What are you doing?" Johnny said.

"Getting in the bath," Jessy replied.

Johnny tried to get up but realized he was stark naked. Stuck and without options, he sat up in the bathtub, wondering what the hell he should do next. He watched Jessy when she reached around like a grand contortionist and undone the laces of her corset. She slithered out of it like a snake shedding its skin; she stood up, showing off her curvy figure, with everything perfect in all the right places. She proudly showed off her milky white flesh.

"Look, we don't have much water around here, so sometimes, we gotta share," Jessy stated.

She strode back and forth near the iron tub in a playful tease. Johnny drank in all her assets. Jessy moved to the other side of the enormous tub. Johnny grinned at her boldness. She climbed in and sat in the bathtub across from Johnny.

"So, what do we do now?" Johnny said.

"As long as I get what I want, you'll get yours," Jessy replied.

Jessy took Johnny's left hand, put his hand under the water, and slid up to him. A ripple arose from the water between them. Jessy's body shuddered with a gasp and a resounding moan of pleasure. The ripples in the water became more vigorous and rhythmic. With Johnny's hand never rising, they kissed, groped, and fondled each other as the sun's soft light escaped into the horizon.

FOUR

ALONZO RODE UP TO THE LARGE RANCH HOUSE IN THE darkness. He dismounted his horse, grabbed his saddle bag, slung it over his right shoulder despite his wounded hand throbbing in pain, and ran inside. He witnessed a large party in the great room of the ranch house where Jericho Jackson, a tall, rawboned man who, despite his rugged countenance, looked far younger than his age of forty-five would indicate. He was holding court in the center of the room. He wore a costly suit that made him a dashing figure. In reality, he was the polar opposite, but he put on a gentleman's act and airs.

Alonzo stared at Jericho, who conversed with two men. Jericho saw the front door open, scanned the room, and met eyes with Alonzo. He noticed his bloodied right hand.

"Would you excuse me, gentlemen?" said Jericho.

Jericho came toward Alonzo, pushed him into the foyer, and closed the large French doors, sealing himself and Alonzo from the party's prying eyes. Jericho grabbed Alonzo's wounded hand and shook it. Alonzo nearly lost his saddle bag off his shoulder.

"What in the hell are you doin' here? You know I got

guests!" Jericho barked.

"I know! I know! Can you let go of my hand?" Alonzo yelped.

Jericho let go of Alonzo's hand. The wound, though superficial, ran red down his appendage—a small flowing creek of gore. Alonzo put his free hand under the stream in an attempt to staunch the bleeding.

"What in the hell happened to your hand?" Jericho said.

"Some drifter in Prosperity shot it," hissed Alonzo.

Jericho took a handkerchief from his suit pocket and wiped his hand. He threw it at Alonzo, who wrapped his right hand while wiping up his left. The pristine white handkerchief became no more. Alonzo's vital fluid bled through.

"What drifter?"

"I don't know who he is. Never saw him before."

"I thought you were going to town with your brother and some of the men?"

"We did."

"And where in the hell are they?"

"They're… they're dead."

"Dead? What in the hell do you mean they're dead? All of them? How?"

"This stranger and his horse killed them."

"What? His horse? You're either drunk or crazy."

"After what I witnessed, wish I was any of those."

"My office. I don't want people to hear you talkin' all crazy."

Jericho and Alonzo walked down the foyer to one of the walls where a bookcase stood. Jericho pushed on a shelf on the bookcase. The bookcase swung open, and a hallway was revealed. Jericho hastily ushered Alonzo through the door with a gesture of shooing away a fly. Jericho closed the bookcase, and the two men walked down what looked like a never-ending hallway. At the end of the hallway stood a large door. Jericho opened the door to reveal a vast office with a large desk surrounded by wooden chairs and a large Victorian Chesterfield Leather Sofa. One of Jericho's bodyguards stood by the door with a massive bodyguard seated on the large leather sofa. It made it look like a chair with zero room for any other occupant—a literal mountain range of a man. Jericho shut the door and unwrapped Alonzo's hand.

"Nicked you a bit. You'll live," Jericho scolded. He let go of the handkerchief. "Now, what's this nonsense of my men bein' dead and one of 'em bein' killed by a horse?"

"We were in Jim's Saloon and told the guy to get out of town by sundown."

"And?"

"Bart went up to the guy's horse and started messing around with it. The horse clamped down on Bart's arm and took it clean off." Alonzo grimaced. He played the scenario through his mind. This wasn't good for his sanity.

"You expect me to believe that?" Jericho snarled.

"Bart staggered back," Alonzo said. "The horse kicked him square in the head, killin' him."

Jericho and the bodyguards laughed at Alonzo's tall tale. Jericho trusted Alonzo because he was honest—strange but honest.

"I've heard some batshit stories in my time, but this one had to be the best," Jericho chuckled.

"Ain't no story. That horse killed my brother!" Alonzo roared. He wanted someone, anyone, to believe him.

"You- you had me goin' on that one," said Jericho. He gasped and held his side in pain from laughter.

Alonzo went to the saddlebag and pulled out Bart's appendage severed at the forearm. He held it out to Jericho and his bodyguards. The men pulled away from the gruesome member, knowing that it was Bart's — Alonzo Clanton, as honest as ever.

"How's it goin' now?" Alonzo growled.

"Jesus Christ!" Jericho cried. "Put that thing away! It's a good thing I caught you in the foyer. The last thing I need is a party full of people goin' plumb loco!"

Alonzo gently put the severed arm back into the saddlebag as one would place a priceless artifact in a glass case and closed the saddlebag. Jericho breathed out a sigh of relief. He never wanted to see that arm again, not ever!

"Suppose I believe that's your brother's arm, and this guy's horse killed him," Jericho stated. "Where are the rest of my men?"

"They were all gunned down in the street," Alonzo said.

"All of 'em?"

"All of 'em."

"One man?"

"One man. With one gun. A six-shooter."

"That's impossible."

"He did it with a trick I ain't never seen anyone do ever," said Alonzo. He shook his head to remove what he'd witnessed from his memories.

"So why didn't he kill you?" Jericho asked.

"He shot my shootin' hand and told me to have Jerry come and see him," Alonzo flatly replied.

Jericho's anger rose. He advanced upon Alonzo and punched him flush on the nose. The heavy thud of his right cross flattened the cartilage briefly. The nose snapped back to its original shape. A trickle of crimson emerged out of each nostril.

"Don't you ever call me by that goddamn name!" bellowed Jericho. "Makes me sound common! I ain't common!"

Alonzo reached for his nose. It looked like one of those blood-letting days for Alonzo. He had experienced these crimson-colored days on his person before, but usually from Jericho's enemies, not from the man himself.

"I'm just tellin' ya what he told me! I just thought he—"

"I don't need you to do the thinkin' for me!"

Jericho threw another white handkerchief at Alonzo.

"So, what does this stranger look like?" Jericho asked.

"He's got this outfit on like he stepped out of a circus or somethin'," Alonzo replied. He placed the handkerchief and clamped down on his nose. "He's tall, skinny, black hair and a black bushy beard like he's hidin'," Alonzo replied through the blood-soaked hanky.

"Could be some trouble. I have to get back to this party. Max, what do you think?"

The giant mountain range rose. His extra-large hand stroked his long, scraggly, dark brown beard on his extra-large face mapped with scars, a product of untreated acne and multiple scraps where the other guy fared far worse.

"You know I like to be called Ironclad," he rumbled.

"Fine… Ironclad. What do you think?" Jericho pressed.

"Sounds like easy work. I expect the usual fee," Ironclad replied.

"All right, all right. As long as the job gets done. Bring a body part back so I know the job is done," Jericho demanded.

"I'll bring you his head." Ironclad smiled. His face broke into a smile that showed off a decayed pair of choppers.

"Fine… and take him with you," Jericho replied, pointing at Alonzo.

"But my hand. I'm hurt pretty bad," Alonzo whined.

"You're gonna be hurt a lot worse if you don't go with him," growled Jericho.

"We're leaving tonight," Ironclad stated.

"Get cleaned up and get going," Jericho snarled at Alonzo. "Don't come back until he's out of town one way or another!"

Jericho exited the office and slammed the office door, ending their conversation. The wheels of Johnny's destruction had begun to turn.

FIVE

S THE SUN ROSE IN THE SKY AND SHONE DOWN UPON Prosperity, Johnny and Jessy got dressed. Johnny was in his new clothes, and Jessy was wearing her untied corset.

"Let me see ya," Jessy said. Johnny showed off his new duds. "Like they were made for ya."

"What'd ya do with my old get-up?" Johnny asked.

Jessy guided Johnny to the balcony. They approached the rail, Jessy put her hand over the balcony, indicated something in the sand. Johnny looked down and saw the remnants of his clothes smoking in a hole in ashes. Johnny's brows raised in surprise.

"You really did put 'em in a pit and burn 'em," Johnny mused.

"True to my word," Jessy replied.

Jessy turned her back to Johnny and revealed the corset's loose strings hanging about her bare back. She could play the carnival contortionist again, but why when she had a handsome man at her disposal?

"Fasten me?"

Johnny took the loose ends of the strings on the corset and pulled hard. Jessy responded with a moan mixed with pleasure and pain. Which of the two feelings was the dominant one couldn't be determined.

§

Jessy wore a black and red dress that flowed down to her ankles, and Johnny transformed from a carnival act to a man in black. His darkened, sun-drenched skin made him even darker. He walked out of the saloon's swinging doors and onto the porch.

"Johnny One… what is your real name?" Jessy said.

"That is my name," Johnny replied.

"I mean, what is your name? Your- your Christian name."

"I don't know if I even had one."

"Everyone's got one."

"I've always been called Johnny One. Even if I had another name, I don't remember it."

The undertaker, Angus Stillman, was a tall, slim, elderly man in his sixties. His white hair shot out of his wide-brimmed hat, and he had a short, well-kept beard on his cheeks that were hollowed due to his failing teeth. He circled the street like a scavenger with a rotted buffet. He measured out some of the dead bodies that Johnny had killed the day before with a long, white fabric tape measure and shooed away the turkey vultures and Rough-Legged Hawks that gathered and picked at the flesh of the dead men.

"Does it matter?" Johnny asked.

"No, guess not," Jessy replied.

"We're all strangers to someone in the end," Johnny

quipped.

Johnny stepped off of the saloon porch, into the street, and approached Angus. The old man never looked back as the sand made a crunch each time his boot landed. He sensed that Angus was a man who not only took his work seriously. His focus never wavered with his measuring, but he felt unnerving joy about his profession.

"You must be the undertaker 'round here. Seen you haul off a few bodies yesterday."

Angus finished measuring a body and looked up at Johnny. His craggy, weather-worn face was the model of this dry and unforgiving land. His milky light blue eyes were set deeply into his oversized head. His irises were black as the darkest night. Johnny felt his orbs looking clear into his soul.

"Mmm-hmm," Angus mumbled.

"Can you hold the bodies for me? I'm gonna need 'em," Johnny said.

Angus forced a smile through his thin lips and rubbed his thumb against his fingers, signifying a 'money' gesture. Johnny's grin widened, and he returned the gesture to Angus. This ancient man had few words, but his mind was as sharp as anyone's.

"So how 'bout it?" Johnny pressed.

Angus shook his head and pointed to the sun to indicate the heat, and then he pointed to the various birds he'd been ineffectively shooing as they continued to pick and pluck at the gore and organs of the fallen men.

"Tell ya what," countered Johnny. "How 'bout puttin' them in shallow graves so I can dig 'em up later?"

Angus nodded in compliance and managed a grin

upon his misshaped face. Johnny surmised that he was an ally and wasn't afraid of nothing and no one. *Why would he? This man would frighten the hell out of anyone!*

"I'll make it worth your while," said Johnny.

Angus shook his head, took out his fabric tape measure, and measured Johnny from the middle of his hat, where the crown of his head rested, to the bottom of his boots. Johnny was unsure what Angus was doing. Angus measured Johnny from his left shoulder to his right. After Johnny's measurements commenced, Angus opened his mouth and exposed a mixture of missing and rotting teeth. Johnny nodded with a half-smile, realizing what this undertaker was up to.

"For you," said Angus. His voice creaked like a door hinge in dire need of oiling.

Angus walked away from Johnny. A large hand grabbed Johnny's gun from the holster. The other large hand pushed Johnny hard in the back. Johnny fell in the street. He rolled over to his back and, through the red haze of sand, recognized who had pushed him down.

"Maximillian Stumpf, AKA Ironclad," declared Johnny.

"And you must be the stranger everyone's talkin' about," rumbled Ironclad.

Johnny got up off the ground and reached for his empty holster. He saw that Ironclad had his gun engulfed in his gigantic hand.

"You won't be needin' this toy," Ironclad smirked. He threw the gun at Alonzo. "Jericho says that you're bein' a notorious pain in his backside."

"Oh, I ain't nearly as notorious as you, Mr. Stumpf.

You're known all over this territory."

"And you know why they call me Ironclad?"

"Why, sure I do. You're as big as a ship. Maybe bigger 'cause you sure are bigger than your sketches, Mr. Stumpf."

"You can have the honor of calling me Ironclad."

"Well, I indeed am honored."

"I want you to know my name when you have your last breath 'cause I'm the one who's gonna kill ya. Maybe I'll have a little fun with your girlfriend when I'm done with ya."

"And we were getting along so well."

Jessy ran off into the saloon. Johnny and Ironclad squared off. They grabbed each other's arms and tried to ne-gotiate leverage. Johnny broke free from Ironclad's grip and started to land rights and lefts into Ironclad's abdomen and ribcage. Each blow proved ineffective while Ironclad stood tall and comically let Johnny land his futile body shots.

"Didn't know you were slummin' for Jerry," Johnny said.

"Ain't slummin' if ya gettin' paid," replied Ironclad.

Ironclad threw an uppercut flush on Johnny's chin. It rocked Johnny's head back like a lid on a jack-in-the-box, lifted him clean off his feet — gone airborne.

"And it's Jericho," Ironclad said.

Gravity came for Johnny. He landed with a giant *thud*. Ironclad rushed toward him. Johnny threw a handful of sand straight into Ironclad's face. Ironclad was temporarily blind-ed. He squatted down and desperately searched for Johnny, but the effort proved useless.

Johnny whistled at Ironclad. Ironclad rose from his squatted position. Johnny emerged from the dust to hit him square in the throat with his fist. Ironclad bent over, held his throat, and gasped from the assault. Johnny turned from the colossus and glared at Alonzo.

"Told ya I wanted to see him personally, but you brought him instead," Johnny growled.

"He sent me, and I obliged," Ironclad snarled.

"I see," Johnny said. He felt his temperature rising. He turned to Ironclad, annoyed at his interruption.

"You ain't never gonna see him no way," Ironclad replied. He coughed as he recovered from the assault to his throat.

"He's evil and owes me," Johnny said.

"So am I, and don't give a shit," Ironclad replied.

Ironclad rushed Johnny, lowered his shoulder, and rammed it into Johnny's chest. Ironclad knocked Johnny over, stomped, and ran through Johnny. Johnny tried to reach his feet but was pulled up by the shirt.

"Looks like I'm going to add you to my pile," Johnny said.

Ironclad hammered Johnny with his right hand. Johnny, his face bloodied by the punch, remained upright. Ironclad still held him tightly by the shirt.

"The only pile you're gonna get is a pile of sand they're gonna dump over your grave!" Ironclad roared.

Ironclad released Johnny's shirt and cracked him with a left hook. Johnny spun around from the force of the punch. Ironclad grabbed Johnny from behind in a bear hug.

Johnny threw his head backward and smashed it into Ironclad's face. Ironclad released Johnny from his clutches and reached for his face. Johnny staggered back and tried to catch his breath as he viewed Alonzo again. As Johnny approached Alonzo, Ironclad grabbed him in a bear hug from behind once more, taking advantage of the distraction. Ironclad kept his head back this time, arched his back, and began to thrust his pelvis forward.

"I'm gonna break you in half!" Ironclad bellowed.

Johnny's head never moved from the center of his shoulders as he lifted the back of his right boot to the fingers on his right hand. He reached down from the long steel shank to the shimmering rowel of his rock grinder spur on his boot. He spun the spur with his index finger and it charged into life like a buzz saw in hyper-drive. He lifted the spinning rowel and shoved it into Ironclad's groin.

The rowel ground into Ironclad, ripping up the scrotum, testicles, and penis. The gore streamed down his legs, staining his faded blue denim jeans.

Ironclad tried to release Johnny, but Johnny's strength bordered on the uncanny. He held Ironclad's arms and moved him closer to his backside as the rowel continued with its carnage.

Ironclad fell to his knees. The rowel stopped, contented with its destruction. Johnny placed his boot heel on Ironclad's chest and pushed. Ironclad fell to the ground, helpless as a newborn child. Johnny turned around and stood over him.

"How-how in hell did you—" said Ironclad. He gurgled—the blood streamed out from his mouth.

CRACK!

Johnny slammed his boot heel into the giant man's skull. It split down the center of his head, and both halves fell into the dust on each side. Brain, blood, and gore spilled out. It stained the sand an even deeper red, along with a fountain of crimson that bubbled and rose out of the various openings within Ironclad's face. It surpassed the stream from his groin.

Johnny felt the ichor upon his face and untied the kerchief from his neck that revealed a deep rope burn scar upon his neck. Jessy fought through the crowd around the saloon and came out with a rifle. She witnessed the aftermath. Johnny stood over the bloodied, dead body of Ironclad. Like the rest of the townsfolk, she saw the scar around Johnny's neck. He wiped the blood from his face with the kerchief and walked up to Alonzo.

"Gun..."

Alonzo, with an extreme case of the shakes, handed Johnny his gun. Johnny put the gun in his left hand and, with his right hand, started to move the cylinder. It made a near — deafening 'click-click-click' sound in Alonzo's haunted mind.

"Is- is he dead?" Alonzo stammered.

Johnny stopped clicking the cylinder, turned back to Ironclad, and swiveled back to Alonzo.

"Well, you don't see him movin', do ya?" Johnny replied.

Angus squealed like a pig at a trough and kneeled by the body. Johnny cocked his head toward Angus.

"Why don't you ask him? He's the expert."

"How did you do—"

"You're askin' an awful lot of questions."

Johnny put the gun to the forehead of Alonzo and squeezed the trigger. The gun clicked harmlessly.

"Must have not loaded it. Or maybe I half-loaded it. I

don't remember."

Johnny cocked the hammer of the gun, still trained on Alonzo's forehead. Alonzo's brow broke into a sweat of fear, and he had no idea why. *Jesus, it's not like this is the first time some fool pointed a damn gun in my face, so why in the hell do I feel so yellow? Who the fuck is this guy?*

"Now I got a question for you. What's it gonna take to get Jerry to come and see me?" Johnny said. His tone was calm but tinged with anger. It broke Alonzo from his thoughts.

"I- I don't know," Alonzo replied. He tried to suppress his shaking.

"Well, that ain't no kinda answer."

Johnny squeezed the trigger. The gun clicked harmlessly. Johnny hoped that this deadly roulette on Alonzo would have come with a bullet. That would have ended this annoying man's life, but being stuck with a useful idiot must be fate.

"Your lucky day," Johnny mused. He pulled his gun away from Alonzo's forehead. "Now you tell Jerry there are two ways this can go. He can come and see me like he was supposed to, or I can see him, which he won't want me to do. So, what's it gonna be?"

"I- I'll tell him."

"You do that. Do it right this time. No more people. No more you, Ironclad, no one. Understand? Go."

Alonzo turned, ran to his horse, mounted it, and rode out of town. Johnny watched Alonzo depart; a flashback rushed into his head. The day he would give anything to forget…

SIX

Johnny and Archer were at the camp with their covered wagon and various horses before the show started. They were getting ready for the show. Johnny played with his gun. He pulled it in and out of the holster and aimed it all over God's creation.

"Johnny, take it easy," Archer said. "Save it for the show."

"Sorry," Johnny trembled. "Just a bit nervous… always am."

"You'll be fine, as always. You're the best damn shot I've ever seen. Best shootist ever."

"Really?"

"May God strike me right here," Archer declared as he pointed to the center of his forehead, "If I ain't tellin' you the God's truth."

"I don't think I'm all—"

"Why do you think I put you as the last act? Gotta save the best—"

A gang of men walked through the town. They were out of focus in Johnny's head. They moved closer and closer to Archer and Johnny.

§

A loud murmur from the crowd snapped Johnny out of his flashback. Johnny walked toward Ironclad's body. He saw a vision of Archer lying in the sand with his mouth agape, his dead eyes open. A bullet hole rested in the middle of his forehead, and blood dripped down his face. Johnny moved toward Archer. Archer's mouth moved while his other features remained unchanged.

"Gotta give 'em a show," Archer's mouth whispered with a smile. "Always gotta be better than the next. Leave 'em wanting more. Got it?"

Johnny turned away from Archer, his eyes drifting towards where they set up camp when they blew into this town too many years ago.

§

Blurred men came into focus in Johnny's mind. It showed a much younger version of Jericho; his wrinkles and grey had lessened with his age in his early thirties. A giant cluster of men joined him as they drew their guns and started shooting. One of the bullets hit Archer square in the head. His mouth slipped from the loudhailer, and his lifeless body fell to the ground. The bullet killed him instantly. Johnny turned to the gang member who killed Archer, pulled his gun, and, in one quick motion, shot him, putting a bullet straight through his chest.

Johnny moved to Archer and checked if there were any signs of life. He shook him and then stared into Archer's open and lifeless eyes. Johnny touched his forehead with his fingers, circling gently around the hole where the bullet had entered. *God didn't strike you there… a man did,* thought Johnny as he closed Archer's eyes. He pulled two silver dollars from his pocket and placed them upon his eyes.

"For the fare, my friend," Johnny whispered like a solemn prayer to his dead mentor and the father he never had.

§

Johnny pinched his nose and the corners of his eyes to stem the tears that formed in them. He never saw the point in grieving the dead. He knew that our time would end at any time, and there may be a better world than this one when the mortal coil has shuffled off. He turned from the daymare, and Angus came into view, measuring Ironclad's body with his fabric measuring tape. Johnny returned to where Archer was lying in the sand, but his presence had disappeared. Johnny and Angus' eyes met. Johnny recovered his senses from his ghost-filled daydream.

"Not today, old man," Johnny smirked.

With his right hand, Angus tapped the chest pocket on his suit jacket, indicating that he still had his measurements. Johnny leaned over to Angus and signaled with the two fingers on his right hand—a 'come here' gesture. Angus understood and leaned over to Johnny. Johnny cupped his hand and whispered into Angus' ear. Angus nodded with each whisper. Johnny withdrew his cupped hand and looked back at where Alonzo had departed from the town. A flashback didn't return; all that was seen was sand and dust. Johnny pulled a fresh kerchief from his pocket and tied it around his neck.

§

Johnny entered the store and approached a hand-carved, oversized brown oak counter with Cyrus standing behind it. Cyrus cleaned the top with a darkened vinegar-filled rag, which caused a sour smell to permeate the store.

"You're full of surprises," Cyrus said. "Never thought you would beat that mountain, much less kill him."

"Lucky shot in the right spot, I guess," Johnny replied.

"You're right about the spot. Not sure about the rest of that, and I'm not sure I wanna know."

"You don't."

"So, what can I help you with?"

"I think my gun needs a bit of cleanin', Johnny said. He put his gun on the counter. "Alonzo might have done somethin' to it."

"I can do that for ya."

Cyrus picked up the gun and examined its cylinder. His eyes moved down to the trigger and saw a smaller lever on the side of the gun below the cylinder and above the firing mechanism. Cyrus pulled the smaller lever, and the cylinder ejected from the gun.

"Damnedest thing I ever saw," Cyrus mumbled.

"Had it done," Johnny replied.

"By who? Never saw a gun like this before."

"I did."

"Well, if you know how to alter a gun, you would know how to clean one."

"I do," said Johnny.

"You ain't here for a gun cleaning."

"I'm not," Johnny replied.

"Why do I get the feelin' it's somethin' I ain't gonna wanna talk about?"

"That day. About a dozen years ago or so."

Cyrus slammed his fist on the counter. His hand turned red from Cyrus' self-assault. It matched his face with the same color of anger.

"Damn! I shoulda known it was somethin' like that you came here for!"

"You were here?"

"No. But Jessy was. She would know more than I do, although I heard plenty. Came two years after."

"What did she say about it?"

"Nothin'. Nobody can get nothin' outta her, but that won't stop people talkin' about it."

"What do they say?" Johnny asked.

"A little too much if ya ask me," Cyrus replied.

"What-do-they-say?" Johnny pressed.

"Why are you so interested?" Cyrus growled. "You act like you were there or somethin'."

"That's 'cause I was," Johnny replied.

"Well, that sure explains a lot," Cyrus said.

"Yep."

"The scar on your neck?"

"Yep," Johnny said.

"And these bastards have been runnin' roughshod all over this town ever since."

"Sure looks that way."

"Oh wait, Jessy… she gave me somethin'."

Cyrus locked the front door, pulled the door shade, and returned to the back of the counter. Cyrus went further into the back of the store. He moved a heavy chair against the wall. It revealed a giant metal safe. Cyrus fiddled with the combination lock, opened the safe, and brought a small, light-colored wooden box. Cyrus returned to the counter and placed the delicate hand-carved box in front of Johnny.

"Smart to put the safe there," Johnny said.

"Well, Jericho's men ain't that smart," Cyrus confessed, "I'm surprised they haven't found it yet, but I'm sure they will someday."

Cyrus opened the small box, and a small, delicate, gold locket was inside it. Johnny gently picked it up and handled the locket. He opened it and saw two small photos of two young children. Johnny circled his thumb around the photo on the left.

"That's gotta be Jessy. Sure as hell looks like her," Cyrus asserted.

Johnny circled his thumb around the photo on the right. It was a black and white ferrotype. Johnny had seen these tintypes before. Cyrus had some of them in his store of various persons frozen in a moment in time—this was one of those times in Jessy's life. Cyrus looked at the image that Johnny's thumb kept circling inside the polished gold locket.

§

Johnny saw Herrick and Olowin. They threw their axes at two of the gang members, who fell to the ground, dead. Herrick and Olowin moved toward the dead bodies and tried to pry their axes out of them, but a part of the horde descended on the twins. The twins tried to fight them off, but there were too many of them, and the gang subdued them. The crowd ran in a fervor of chaos as some of the crew indulged in target practice on the scurrying crowd.

Johnny made his way to the end of the main street, where the covered wagon and his horse resided. He gunned down any gang member who blocked his way. Johnny mounted his horse. He was ready to leave the town but saw Jessy helpless in the carnage. Johnny cursed under his breath, turned his horse around, and rode towards Jessy. He unloaded upon any man that got in his way.

Johnny leaned over and scooped up Jessy. He held her side saddle as he rode towards the general store's porch, away from the mayhem and chaos in the streets. He arrived at the porch and set Jessy on it. Johnny snapped the reins and rode his horse out of town. He shot and killed anyone who had the nerve to stop him.

§

"Don't know who that is," Cyrus rumbled. "A brother, maybe? She didn't say she had a brother. Locket's her mother's, I think. You can take it if you want. She wanted me to sell it, but I couldn't bring myself to do it."

Johnny stopped the thumb circling and held the open locket with the younger Jessy and the unknown male staring up at him. *She was more of a stranger than he was,* thought Johnny when he snapped the locket shut.

SEVEN

ESSY OPENED THE DOOR. JOHNNY STOOD IN THE MIDDLE OF her room, holding the locket between his right thumb and forefinger. He left it to dangle and spin in the sunlight. She recognized this trinket of her past.

"Where in the hell did you get that?" Jessy demanded. She was met with silence. "I told that damn fool to sell that thing."

"Said he couldn't do it," Johnny replied.

"Damn him to hell for keeping it and to you for taking it!" she yelled.

Johnny opened the locket, showing Jessy the two pictures inside. Johnny pointed to the photo on the right. He knew it was Jessy, but he wanted to hear it from her mouth.

"You?"

"Yeah," said Jessy. "I was about nine. My mother always wore the locket. She never took it off."

Johnny pointed to the photo on the left. Confident it was a sibling and none of his business, he ventured to pry.

"Brother?"

"Yeah… Jacob… about five years," Jessy replied.

"That day?" Johnny questioned.

"No. He died about a year after the picture. That was ten years before that day ever occurred. Doc said typhoid. My father and I tried to get a picture of us without Jacob, but she wouldn't have it," Jessy replied. She fought the tears that welled up in her eyes.

Johnny closed the locket with a click and held it by the chain, allowing it to spin and dangle from his hand. He stared gently into Jessy's dark brown eyes.

"Take it."

"I don't want it… any of it."

Johnny pried Jessy's fingers and placed the locket in her palm. Once the locket was in her hand, he took her fingers and delicately closed her hand over it.

"That day…" Johnny whispered.

"I don't wanna talk about it. I only want to remember the good of that day," Jessy replied. Her voice trembled like a wagon over an uneven trail.

"You can't, and you know it."

"Everyone wants to talk about it."

"So I've heard."

"Including you."

"That's why I'm here."

"I was hoping you would. Took you long enough."

"Almost didn't."

"Scared?"

"Something like that."

Jessy fidgeted with the locket, turning the ancient heirloom in her palm and rubbing it. She didn't want to ask the next question, but, like a dormant volcano coming to life, it emerged out of her like hot lava.

"But you were gonna run," Jessy stated.

"Didn't feel like it was my fight," Johnny replied.

"But you shot and killed some of 'em,"

"Just to keep 'em off me," Johnny said.

"But your friends.... "

"Couldn't have saved 'em if I tried. "

Here come those memories again in my head, Johnny rumbled in his mind. *Those goddamn memories!*

§

Around their covered wagons and horses, Johnny loaded ammunition into his gun while Herrick and Olowin sharpened their axes. Johnny began fidgeting with the bullets, loading and unloading each chamber. Herrick and Olowin shook their heads.

"Johnny… relax," Herrick said.

"Yeah… you're making even me nervous," Olowin added.

"Sorry," Johnny apologized.

"You'll be fine," Herrick assured.

"Always are," Olowin said.

"Thanks."

"Hey, can I ask you something?" Herrick asked.

"Sure," Johnny replied.

"The tattoos. How'd you get 'em?"

"They used to be fake. I decided to get 'em done permanent."

"Didn't they hurt? They sure looked like it."

"Like hell."

"Why did you decide to do that?" Herrick queried.

"Instead of getting into character, I want to be the character. I wanted to do and be this my whole life."

"But you're a kid," Olowin said.

"I've done it for years. Ever since I was little," Johnny replied.

"Like you were born into it," Herrick mused.

"I guess it was my calling. My choice." Johnny sheepishly grinned.

"Something we never had," Olowin said.

"Something we ain't never gonna have," Herrick grumbled.

"What do you mean?"

"Johnny…" Olowin sighed.

"You're young but not stupid," Herrick stated.

"C'mon, now," Johnny protested.

"Look at us and look at you," Olowin replied.

"We're what they call Lakota, and you're… whatever you are," Herrick said.

"Well, I'm- I'm white," Johnny replied.

"Exactly!" Olowin exclaimed.

Johnny chewed on the twin's words. He couldn't imagine what these two men had experienced throughout their lives. He had heard about some of the atrocities that the natives suffered at the hands of the white man but never witnessed them.

"I see," Johnny said. He nodded and quickly changed the subject. "Ain't you two from around these parts?"

" A bit northeast from here. What they call the Dakota Territory," Herrick answered.

"Got family there?"

"Used to," Olowin mumbled.

"Used to?"

"Before the white man came…" Herrick said. He continued to sharpen his axe in a rhythmic, hypnotic beat…

§

It was the spring of 1877, the year of our lord in the Black Hills in the aftermath of the Lakota's victory over U.S. Troops at Little Bighorn. Herrick and Olowin, in their mid-thirties, were walking around what used to be their home and seeing the destruction's aftermath. Olowin heard of American troops that raided their land as revenge toward his people. He cursed himself for getting to the land in the spring and not sooner, as did Herrick, who knew there was trouble and that the white man's raids were terrible but didn't know how terrible. They found out.

Herrick and Olowin searched through the remnants of tipis, smashed pottery, and animal skins. The twins moved around their lost land. They found desiccated bodies and skeletons of their people, most of the bodies picked clean by the various scavengers, both man and beast. The bodies with flesh that remained on their bones gave off a putrid stench that gagged both of the brothers. They knew more people were in their village. They looked around for survivors. None were found.

§

"There wasn't anyone to bury the dead. No medicine man nor women to conduct ceremonies for our dead. That's why we don't have a choice," Herrick said.

"Couldn't you go, do something else?" Johnny asked, trying to ease his heavy heart's guilt and stop his gorge from rising.

"Go where? To the reservation, where the rest of our people have gone? And do what? There is nothing to go to," said Olowin.

"Smallpox, starvation, and soldiers… our people are gone… all gone," Herrick replied.

"I- I'm sorry… I- I don't know what to say."

"White people have destroyed and shaped us into what we are," Olowin stated.

"And we'll be killed by them, too," Herrick replied.

"Why do you say that?"

"They killed our family, so why not us?" Herrick said.

Johnny thought about what these men had said to him. Was what Herrick was saying a signpost of things to come? Johnny shuddered at the thought of these powerful men's demise. He'd heard of a new act called fortune telling, where a seer looked into your future. He never witnessed it firsthand and with such surety from the twins.

"Hey, we've decided to give you something," Olowin declared.

"What is it?"

Olowin looked at Herrick. Herrick went over to the large saddlebag on his horse. He pulled out a small sack and returned to Johnny and Olowin. He handed Johnny the small sack. Johnny was about to open it, but Olowin put his enormous, meaty hand over the sack.

"Not yet," said Olowin. "You have to promise us something."

"All right."

"Whoever manages to kill us," Herrick said. "We

want our revenge."

"How will I know that?"

"You will."

"I don't know if I can make that promise."

"You have to," Olowin stated. "We have no one left. You're the only one we trust."

"Yeah, you're okay," Herrick added. He made a circle around his face and pointed to each place where Johnny had his tattoos. "Crazy, but okay."

Johnny laughed, and Herrick and Olowin joined in. Their laughter came to a stop as the twins' faces turned stone-faced. Johnny had never seen their demeanor shift so quickly. It had to be serious—deadly serious.

"You trust us, don't you?" Olowin questioned.

"Of course I do," Johnny replied.

"Then promise," Herrick and Olowin said in unison.

"I- I promise."

Johnny held the sack and waited for instructions. They had never given him anything before, so it must be valuable—not money but substance—something the twins held dear.

"Now?" Johnny said.

Herrick and Olowin nodded in the affirmative, and Johnny opened the sack.

§

"Could have tried to save them, but I didn't. Young and self-ish, I guess," Johnny said.

§

Jessy saw Johnny riding away from the town in the middle of an insane melee courtesy of Jericho's gang. She stepped off of the porch of the saloon and onto the street. She was tackled by one of the gang.

§

"I was hopin' you would have stopped them," Jessy exhaled. She turned her passivity into ferocity. "Coward…"

"That's fair," Johnny replied. "My cowardice didn't do me much good anyway…"

§

Johnny rode away from the town to escape the chaos. Jericho saw him and gestured to some of his gang. Jericho and his henchmen rode out of town to catch Johnny. They gained on him. Jericho fired, and the bullet hit the horse›s leg. The horse buckled as the bullet shattered its leg bone. The horse fell to its side on the ground, trapping Johnny underneath.

Johnny struggled to slide himself out from under the horse, but it was futile. The horse's weight was too much; his right leg was pinned underneath. Jericho and the gang stopped and dismounted their horses. Jericho walked to Johnny and drew his gun. He pointed it at Johnny and cocked the hammer. Jericho turned the gun to the horse's head and pulled the trigger.

The horse stopped struggling, and a stream of blood rolled out of the equine's head and clustered in a pool of dark red. Its deadweight pinned down Johnny even more than before. Jericho pointed the gun at Johnny, cocking the hammer. Johnny's struggle renewed in a useless effort to escape from under the horse. Jericho uncocked his gun, pointed the barrel up in the air, and came down with the heel of his boot on Johnny's head, rendering him unconscious.

Johnny's eyes fluttered open and closed. Going in

and out of consciousness, he caught certain things in his vision. His eyes hazily viewed the horse under him, getting further away as some of Jericho's men pulled and dragged him out from under his horse. His eyes closed again.

His eyes opened to see Jericho and his crew slung a rope over a tree and pulled it back up. It revealed a noose on the rope's end. Johnny tried to struggle away, but he was held tight by two of his executioners. His eyes closed once more.

Johnny opened his eyes. He saw Jericho and his clan, who looked up at him. Johnny looked around and realized he was on a tree's high branch. Johnny was pushed and fell from a giant cottonwood tree branch, but the rope around his neck stopped him. Johnny grabbed for the rope but swung uncontrollably from the end of the rope as it pulled taut. The noose strangled him without a reprieve in sight. Johnny's eyes closed for the final time as his world went black.

§

Jessy gently pulled Johnny's kerchief down. It revealed the rope burn scar around his neck.

"This? How did you —"

"I don't know."

§

Johnny opened his eyes and coughed loudly, which, ironically, brought his body back to life. As the coughing subsided, Johnny scanned the area, but Jericho and his hangmen were nowhere to be found. He reached for his throat and felt the burn of the rope around his neck. Still concussed but now breathing normally, he vomited into the sand. After the contents of his stomach emptied, a screaming sound erupted within the insides of his head. With the screaming, a vision flashed in his head —Herrick and Olowin lay dead in the sand. Blood covered them. Johnny covered his head in his hands, still nauseous and in pain, as another vision flashed within his head — Jericho.

Johnny got up from his vomiting and visions. He looked upon his horse, which, by some strange miracle, stood in front of him, alive and breathing. Johnny viewed a lump in the saddlebag, emitting a soft whistle while pushing and moving about the bag as if something had come to life and wanted to get out. The saddle bag's sound and movement stopped, and Johnny scanned the area. He was much further from town and his hanging tree. Unsure if this was his horse or what the hell had happened. He went to his horse, mounted it, and slowly rode away from the area and the town.

§

"Somebody must have cut me down and pulled me away from the tree. Not sure why," Johnny murmured. He turned Jessy's vanity chair around and sat across from her.

"And your horse?"

"Looked like my horse, but it couldn't have been."

"Strange."

"What's stranger is that I was saved for bein' a coward," Johnny said. "Like I said, it didn't do me much good."

"Me neither," Jessy whispered. She rubbed the locket with her thumb, hoping to conjure a spirit or genie that would take her mind off that day…

§

A gang member tackled Jessy. He fell on top of her, hitting the ground with a heavy *thud*. He took his left hand, grabbed the top of her blouse, and began to rip it open, and he started to

71

move his right hand under her skirt.

Jessy desperately tried to gain her bearings as the gang member continued his assault on her. She tried to push him off her, but she was unable to do so. Tears streamed down her face as she turned away from her assaulter while he moved his hips. He slid in his unwelcomed member and poisoned her virgin spring. After he finished his assault on Jessy, he rolled off her, stood up, and reached for his gun to complete his assault with murder, but it wasn't there.

Jessy struggled to sit up from the assault and pointed the gun at him. He advanced toward Jessy. He moved closer while gunshots thundered through the melee. A bullet went clean through her assaulter's head. He fell to the ground; his body twitched slightly and ceased.

Jessy looked around to where the shot came from, but no one was in sight. A stray bullet with its origins unknown had killed her rapist. Jessy got to her feet and advanced upon the dead gang member. She screamed above the din of chaos, pointed the gun at her attacker, and fired into his dead body. Again and again, until the bullets were no more. She screeched in fury and fired the gun. The empty chambers harmlessly clicked away. Her fury ceased. The pulling of the trigger stopped. Jessy walked out of the town. She still held the unloaded gun.

§

"I wanted you to save me... save us," Jessy said. She peered down at her locket.

"Wasn't going to happen that day," mumbled Johnny.

"So now you're back."

"After some time after that day, I continued to perform my act."

Images of the past shot through Johnny's head. He performed his shooting act in another town. He shot his gun at a series of cards flying through the air. Bullets entered the center of the suit on each card.

"Went through a lot of towns."

Various towns and performances floated through Johnny's head like a waking dream. Each performance had aged Johnny with each shot he fired.

"Met a lot of challenges."

His daydream continued, with a series of cards flying through the air. Bullets flew through each suit in a series of shots with a thick fog that obscured the cards. When the fog cleared, Johnny drew his gun and outdrew man after man after man in the street. He gunned them down one by one. A wanted poster was torn down, then another, then another with each man he killed.

"But with every town I went to that day… this town… it never escaped my mind…"

Johnny's haunted mind continued with his performances as he put bullets through cards and men. Johnny continued to age until the series of shots ended, with Johnny being his current age. He held his gun and shot it.

"Every year that went by, it gnawed at me… haunted me 'til my mind couldn't take it anymore… I had to find a way back… I came back for redemption."

"More like revenge," Jessy snorted.

"Revenge… redemption… it all walks the same path."

"You know he'll come," Jessy said.

"He has to," Johnny replied. "He's runnin' out of men."

"He's got way more than you can imagine."

"There'll be no doubt that he'll bring 'em."

"You ain't gonna get no help in this town."

"Don't expect none."

"How can you be so sure of yourself?"

"Look, if I get redemption, this town will start fresh, and I can erase my mistake."

"And if you die?"

"I don't plan on it, but if I do, this is as good a place as any."

Johnny stood up from the chair and took Jessy's arm. Jessy reluctantly rose from the bed.

"Where are we goin'?" Jessy said.

"Outside," Johnny replied. "I need some air."

Jessy stopped Johnny from leading her out of the room. Johnny turned back to her, surprised at her immovable stance. He looked deep into her brown eyes. Water had begun to pool within her lower eyelids.

"C'mon," Johnny gently pleaded, "no tears for me."

Too late—they ran down Jessy's cheeks.

"I-I don't even know why I'm doing this," Jessy wept. "I didn't even cry when my parents died."

"That day..."

Jessy nodded as she opened her hand. It revealed her mother's locket again. She opened the locket once more and looked at the picture of her youth and her long-deceased brother. She would keep this but never wear it. She snapped the locket shut. She promised herself that she would never open it again.

§

Jessy staggered like a being of the undead away from the town. She saw obscured figures lying in the dust in the distance. As she moved closer, the bodies came into focus—two dead bodies that revealed themselves to be her mother and father. Jessy tried to clear her head from the constant trauma. They must have tried to escape and were shot in the chest by Jericho's gang. She kneeled over to the bodies and shook them both, but neither responded. Jessy sobbed and laid her head upon her mother's bosom. She felt something hard against her head. Her grief turned to rage. Rage at her father and mother for not protecting her when she needed them the most. She tore at her mother's dress and ripped open her neckline. What glinted in the sun was the beautiful gold locket. She realized the rough treatment of her mother's clothing. Her rage melted into guilt as she gently lifted her mother's head and unclasped the locket from her neck.

§

"I didn't want anyone, much less those bastards, to get ahold of this," Jessy stated. She stared at her mother's locket. The pain of her past slowly dissipated from her mind.

"They took their lives… they sure as hell weren't going to take anything else."

"Then why did you tell Cyrus to sell it for ya?"

"I wanted to forget… to move on… but—"

"Can't…"

Johnny took the locket from her hand and placed it on the vanity table. These horrible flashbacks and awful reminiscing became too much.

"C'mon… Looks like we could both use some air."

Johnny and Jessy exited the room and entered the outdoors. They left their catastrophic past behind and focused on the potential doom that awaited them.

EIGHT

JERICHO SAT IN A GIANT BLACK LEATHER-BOUND CHAIR behind his matching hand-carved mahogany desk. He smoked a giant cigar that jutted out of his square jaw. Alonzo sat in a simple oaken chair across from Jericho.

"Why do you return at the worst times?" said Jericho between puffs.

"I wanted to tell—"

"And on top of that, bring me the worst news."

"You that—"

"Don't tell me this stranger killed Max!" snarled Jericho.

"Ironclad," Alozo corrected.

"Whatever the hell he wants to be called."

One of Jericho's bodyguards burst into the office. Fear etched upon his melon-like head. Jericho rose from his seat. He threw down his cigar.

"What now?' Jericho barked.

"Someone's comin'," the bodyguard said, his voice trembling and barely audible. "You may wanna come outside and see."

§

Jericho, Alonzo, and a some of the men came out from the front of the house and stood on the porch as a cart pulled by two horses approached the ranch house. The cart moved closer, and Angus Stillman came into view. The cart came to a stop near the ranch house. Angus climbed onto the cart and pushed an enormous, crude wood coffin off the back of his cart, landing with a heavy thud. Angus returned to the driver's seat and threw a hammer and chisel. Angus pointed to the large coffin and then at Jericho.

"For you," Angus said. He gurgled and grinned, showing off his near-toothless maw. He snapped the reins and let out a hearty cackle. The cart left the premises.

"I hate that old man. Gives me the shakes," Jericho trembled.

"Shoulda killed him when I had the chance," spat Alonzo.

"You've had too many chances," Jericho said. He approached the large coffin. "Looks like our stranger sent us a gift. I wanna see what's inside."

Alonzo hadn't moved from his spot—frozen in place. He knew full well what was inside the gigantic wooden overcoat.

"Come on," Jericho growled. "Open it."

"I know what it is," Alonzo replied.

"Open it," Jericho said. "I want to see for myself."

Alonzo hesitated. He did not want to believe that the intruder in Prosperity killed the giant Ironclad. Jericho pulled his gun from his holster. He aimed it at the tools and then at Alonzo. He cocked the hammer on his gun.

"Open," Jericho hissed.

With a tremendous amount of effort, Alonzo managed to pry open the coffin cover, revealing the corpse of Ironclad, complete with his bloodied groin. Where his head used to be was nothing but gore and splintered bone.

Jericho's hand went to his mouth. He'd seen worse mutilations, but this was different as he tried to keep his composure and guts around the men. He blew air out of his lungs to cease his disgust.

"Cover it," Jericho groaned.

Alonzo started to put the cover back on the coffin. A couple of businessmen left the ranch house. One of the businessmen, Arthur Nelson, stepped forward from the group. He was a man of significant height and gangly proportions. His slicked-to-the-side, grayish-black hair that stuck out of his brown derby hat matched his simple, dark brown suit. It displayed him as a man of means. He looked down at Jericho with his gold-rimmed spectacles that glimmered around his clean-shaven face.

"Mr. Jackson, is there a problem?"

Jericho made himself bigger to block their view of the coffin, which would sink his interests if the men caught wind of his troubles.

"No, Mr. Nelson. Just a small issue in town. I'm seeing to it personally," Jericho removed his palm from his face and presented a false smile.

"See that you do," Nelson stiffly replied. "We want to ensure our business dealings with you stay ironclad if you catch my meaning."

Nelson and the other businessmen went back into the ranch house. Jericho knew he had to have this problem fixed—and fast!

"Two things," grumbled Jericho. "One, we did something to this man, and two, we didn't finish the job."

"There's something else," said Alonzo.

"I'm sure there is," Jericho snarled.

"There's some kind of scar around his neck."

"A scar?"

"More like a burn. Looks like a rope burn of some kind."

"Like he's been hanged?"

"Yeah… "

"That tells me nothin'. I've hanged a lot of people."

Alonzo stopped hammering the lid and looked back at Jericho, dumbfounded. Jericho nodded, knowing that his right-hand man had become useless before his eyes.

"Yeah," Jericho growled, "I've thought about it."

Alonzo hammered down on the lid. He didn't want to look at Jericho for fear he would be shot dead. or the thought his men would turn on him and tear him apart at any moment.

"That's enough," grumbled Jericho. "Get this outta my sight."

"Where?" Alonzo said.

"Anywhere!" Jericho exploded. "I don't care where you put this goddamned thing; just get it out of here!"

Alonzo tried to pick up the coffin, which was far too heavy. He wanted to get rid of this death box as fast as humanly possible—out of Jericho's sight.

"Don't just stand there like a bunch of fucking statues!" Jericho bellowed at his men. "Get this thing the hell out of here!"

The henchmen assisted Alonzo. They picked up and carried the enormous coffin.

"And when you get done with that, mount up the horses," Jericho stated, "We're going to pay our stranger a visit."

Alonzo and the gang members moved the coffin and quickly exited, leaving Jericho to himself. Jericho tried his best to control his rage. His jaw clenched, moved his lower jawbone, and ground his teeth.

"You want me... here I come."

NINE

JOHNNY AND JESSY WERE ALONE IN THE MIDDLE OF THE DUST and sand, a reasonable distance from the town. Johnny carried a sack containing several boxes of bullets. Johnny pulled out one of the boxes and grabbed a bunch of bullets. He loaded the cylinder of his gun. He spun the cylinder, shoved the cylinder into place, and placed his gun back into his holster. He loaded bullets into the extra cylinders and shoved them into the left and right sleeves of his shirt and the loops on his holster. He took a deck of playing cards from his shirt pocket and placed the deck of cards in Jessy's hand. Johnny stepped away from Jessy. Jessy took one card from the deck and tapped it against the stack of cards. A faint, metallic *tink* of a sound emanated from the deck.

"Think ya bought enough bullets?" Jessy said.

"Cleaned Cyrus out at the store. Thought I might need them," Johnny replied.

"You thought right."

Jessy playfully tapped the cards with their metal clinking. Johnny grinned at her doing that. He knew his secret would be revealed one day.

"I remember these cards," she said. "Did you make

these?"

"No, I had a photographer do 'em. He did ferrotypes like your locket. I had him cut a bunch of tin into the size of playing cards, and then I would fashion regular cards to the front and back of the tin, cause—"

"—Regular cards would fly off and get blown apart 'cause there just stiff paper," Jessy stated.

"Right. So when I had someone throw them up in the air, it gave the illusion of a playing card being thrown so a bullet would go through the tin card," Johnny replied. He walked further away from Jessy."The cards weren't real, but the bullets were."

"Did anyone find out about your secret?"

"I had to read every crowd and trust that, in their hearts, they were good people and wouldn't give my trick away, like you. Luck of the draw, I guess."

"I saw that when you were done, the crowd would look at the cards but never pick them up. Has anyone ever done that?"

Well, it was some child that would do it, but I would do something like this," Johnny said, putting his finger to his lips and winking his right eye. He continued to walk a far enough distance from Jessy.

"I know we were getting some air, but why did you drag me out here?"

"So we could talk away from pryin' eyes and, more importantly, pryin' ears," Johnny stated. He created a reasonable distance from her. "Thought we'd have a little fun like we used to, and I could use the target practice."

"I don't want to do this."

"Oh, come on now. Didn't you say you'd never forget that day?"

"Yeah… but for different reasons."

"That makes two of us."

"Do you remember?" Johnny enquired. He faced Jessy, pointing to various places on his bearded face.

"'Course I do, but the bigger question is, am I still a natural?" Jessy said. She fanned out the cards in a playful tease.

A sun flare enveloped Jessy and cast her as the younger Jessy when fate first served them to each other. Sunspots blinded Johnny. When his vision cleared, Jessy returned to her older self.

"Even more…" Johnny replied.

Johnny put his left index finger under his nose and upper lip. Jessy flipped the card over. It revealed the four of spades. She flung the card in the air. Johnny opened fire at the card four times. The card fluttered down and landed on the ground. Four bullet holes were in the center of each spade on the card.

"Damn… dead center in each. More accurate than before."

"I got older," Johnny stated. He took some bullets out of the loops of his holster and re-loaded his gun.

"And better," Jessy replied.

Johnny put his left index finger under his lower lip. Jessy pulled out a card. It flashed the six of hearts. She flung it up in the air. Johnny fired six shots at the card, and the card came down with all six hearts with bullet holes in the center.

"Don't you ever miss?"

"Once in a while."

"Hope you're doing the right thing. Don't want to see old man Angus use those measurements."

"Yeah, me too."

Johnny switched the gun from his right to his left hand. He put his right index finger on his right cheek. Jessy pulled out a card and flipped it toward Johnny. It revealed the two of diamonds. She flung it up, and Johnny fired two shots at the card.

"So, how in the hell is Jericho still here? Thought he would have moved on by now."

"Would you have moved on if you had all the power over this town?"

Johnny milled over the question. Jessy transformed from a young woman filled with innocence to a mature, thoughtful woman who spoke truth with the power of a blacksmith's hammer.

"No… guess not."

"Now he's a businessman."

"Is he?"

"He's in cahoots with all these rich, fancy business-men from out east."

Johnny switched the gun from his left hand to his right hand. He put his left index finger on his left cheek. Jessy pulled out one of the cards—the three of clubs. She flung it into the air. Johnny fired at the card three times before it fell to the ground.

"I see."

"He's tryin' to push us all out. He lies about it, of course."

Johnny re-loaded his gun. He knew that Jericho was an evil man, but as he witnessed every word he heard about this man, he was far worse than he could ever have imagined.

"Of course."

Johnny put his index finger under his lower lip. Jessy pulled out the five of hearts. She flung it into the air. Johnny fired five times at the card before it fell into the sand.

"Why don't you fight back?" Johnny asked. "It's been twelve years."

"He's got too many resources and too many men. The people that have are out there in the cemetery."

Johnny took more bullets out of the loops of his holster and re-loaded his gun.

"And the rest?"

"Too scared."

§

Cyrus straightened the store when Jericho and his men burst through the door. One of the men grabbed Cyrus and slammed him into the wall, knocking merchandise onto the floor.

"Where is he?" Jericho hissed.

"Where is who?" grunted Cyrus.

Jericho nodded to the man holding Cyrus. He struck Cyrus with a solid shot to the face—a vicious right hook. Cyrus' face reddened and crinkled in pain as he waited for another punch, which, to his surprise, never arrived.

"Again... where is he?"

"Who? The stranger? I don't know."

Jericho nodded to the rest of the men. They began their destruction of the store. Pictures were ripped from the walls; their frames smashed when the gang broke them over

86

their knees. Clay pots were swept off the counters and landed on the floor with a crash.

"What are you doing?" cried Cyrus. "Stop! Please stop!"

"I could set fire to this place, and there wouldn't be a damn thing you could do about it," Jericho growled.

"I told you, I don't know! He-he bought some bullets from me and—"

Gunfire echoed in the distance. Jericho and his men froze instantly when an index finger pointed up by Jericho stopped the destruction. He slowly walked to the store's front door. The echo returned.

"There you are..." Jericho seethed. He put his hand on his holster and looked to remove the pestilence that had infected his town.

§

Johnny took the bullets out of the carton and continued to put bullets into the loops of his holster.

"Even you?"

"Even me."

"But I saw you at the bar stickin' a rifle in those bastards' faces."

"I was outta my mind."

"Were ya?"

"Yeah... I- I didn't know what I was doin'."

Johnny continued to switch the gun from his right to his left hand. With his right index finger, he touched underneath his nose. Jessy pulled out a card and showed it to Johnny—the ace of spades. She once again flung the card up in the air. Johnny shot at it before it fell into the sand.

"I don't believe you... and you don't believe it either," Johnny declared.

Jessy's face became a compound of anger and disgust. With a clatter, she dropped the rest of the deck of cards in the sand and walked away from the tin cards and Johnny. She knew he was right but couldn't admit it.

"Running away just like I did," Johnny said.

Johnny grabbed Jessy's arm and pulled her towards him. Jessy, in one motion, took her right knee and smashed it squarely into Johnny's groin. In surprise and shock, Johnny released Jessy's arm and fell to his knees. He held his groin and wheezed like a man riddled with black lung.

"You deserved that."

"Can't say I'm gonna argue with you."

"I've seen too many hard men killed by Jericho and his damn gang."

"Not to mention the hard women and children."

"Yeah... that too... along with my parents."

"Then have your redemption... your revenge."

"Because I'm-not-you," Jessy said.

"No.... you're tougher," Johnny replied. He struggled to reach his feet. He winced and gathered his breath.

Johnny got his bearings from the shot to his nether regions. He started to recuperate but didn't dare go to his family jewels, though he desperately wanted to.

"That was harder than the kick I got Ironclad with," Johnny mused.

"He's dead."

"It was damn close."

"Stop it."

Johnny finally recovered, but when Jessy came to him, he braced for another blow that never came. *Damn! She's tough. Tougher than any of us!*

"I still don't know how you did it." Jessy flatly stated — the gory demise of Ironclad entering her mind.

"Can't say that I know. Guess it was luck or fate or somethin'."

"I don't believe your nonsense... don't think you do either," Jessy replied. She returned to the deck of cards in the sand, picked them up, and collected them in her hand.

"I don't want to see any more killing... I've seen enough."

"You're gonna see more. Cyrus talked about statehood for this territory, right?"

"Yeah."

"You're never gonna get statehood without law and order... at least not his kinda law and order."

Johnny gently took the cards out of her hand and threw them as they landed into the sand with a *thunk*. Then, like some grand plan, a wind blew hard and buried them deep into the desert.

"We should get back; they'll be waitin'," Johnny spoke through the wind. He was mixed with anticipation and fear. He didn't want to deal with this, but sometimes, a man has to do what he has to do.

TEN

JERICHO AND HIS MEN LEFT THE GENERAL STORE AND MET with the other gang members on the main street. Jericho directed his men to go to the entrance of the town to meet up with Johnny. Cyrus emerged from his store, took a kerchief, and wiped off his bloodied face. When he saw the trouble, he walked back into his store. He looked for anything to help his newfound friend, but with Jericho's arsenal and resources, he knew his help would prove useless.

Cyrus looked around at the destruction of his once immaculate store. He began to clean up the mess Jericho's men inflicted upon it. Something caught his eye. Inside a smashed picture frame was a tintype of a young man and woman dressed in wedding attire. It was a young Cyrus and his wife on their wedding day. Boot marks marred the metal. It had been scratched in various places. Cyrus tried desperately to clean the ferrotype and fix the frame, but all his efforts were futile. This artifact was the only remains of his wife.

Captain of all these men of death, Doc Harris called it. His fancy name for consumption. They moved from a comfortable existence in New York to this godforsaken desert upon Harris' recommendation that the dry heat would help her condition. He was wrong. *Too far gone* was Doc Franklin's excuse for her failing condition. She died in isolation, away from me and the rest of the town, and in a wink of an eye, their hope of a long life of matrimony ended before it even began. *God, I miss her so much!*

Cyrus' sadness turned into a wave of extreme anger, an emotion he hadn't experienced for decades when various dark deeds ruled his life…

§

Johnny and Jessy returned to town. The wind whistled around them like an unknown omen. The end was coming—one way or another.

"Sorry, I kneed you like I did," Jessy winced.

"Nah. I shouldn't have grabbed ya like I did."

"You called me a coward."

"And I paid for it. It still hurts."

"Dented your armor, eh?"

"Hey, we're all vulnerable… you, I, everybody."

They walked up the town, and Jericho and his gang awaited them.

"Looks like your armor's gonna be dented a hell of a lot more," Jessy stated as Jericho and his bodyguards drew their guns.

"Yep. Sure looks that way," Johnny mused. He stepped ahead of Jessy. "You need to get out of here. He wants me."

"John—"

"I said I would handle this. Now go!"

Jessy stepped away. Johnny advanced on Jericho and his men. She knew he had no chance of defeating them. Despite his bravado, he would be just another headstone.

"So, you're the man who wants to see me," Jericho smirked.

"And you're the man who finally shows up," Johnny replied.

Jericho gestured to his aides. Some pointed their guns at Johnny while the others advanced toward him. They grabbed each of Johnny's arms and pulled them behind his back. Johnny didn't resist, even when Jericho came upon him.

"Think ya brought enough men with ya, Jerry?" Johnny mocked.

Jericho hit Johnny square in the mouth. He shook his hand in the aftermath of the blow.

"I've been wanting to do that for some time," Jericho said. He tried to hide his pain and not turn his expression into a grimace. That never would have happened when he was younger. He had gone soft—far too soft.

Johnny turned his head, spit into the sand, and cracked a bloody smile at Jericho. Johnny felt the man's punch, but its strength ebbed significantly. Jericho had lost his touch, his bite—aging before his eyes.

"You killed enough of my men, especially one of my best. I got your delivery," Jericho growled. He nodded to his allies. They escorted Johnny into town.

"Where are we goin'?" Johnny said.

"I want to know who I'm dealing with. I have some idea now that I see ya, but I want to be sure."

Johnny, Jericho, and his men marched Johnny down the main street, and a crowd gathered along the main street. The group stopped and turned Johnny towards one of the storefronts, whose sign boldly declared, 'Barber Shop.' Jericho's gang members pushed Johnny through the barbershop door. Jericho was about to enter the barbershop when some of his henchmen stepped up to protect him.

"Wait outside. Don't let anyone else in here," Jericho commanded. His aides, who weren't escorting Johnny into the shop, stood guard outside the barbershop like stone statues. Jericho entered.

They shoved Johnny into the barber chair. The barber, Thaddeus Mudd, is an average-looking man of forty-five. His only distinguishing features were his perfectly coiffed, wavy, ink-black hair and the most fantastic handlebar mustache anyone had ever seen. He was shaving an elderly man in the other barber chair. He glided elegantly around the man's face with a straight razor. A towel resided on Thaddeus' left shoulder. Jericho's hand came down hard on Thaddeus' toweled shoulder, which nearly sliced off his customer's cheek. He spun Thaddeus towards him.

"Shave him," said Jericho.

"But Thad's not done with me yet," said the elderly man.

"He is now," Jericho stated. He and his gang pulled their guns in response to the man's stupid reply.

The man scampered out of the chair, toweled off his half-shaven face, and ran out of the barbershop. The fool should have known better to have challenged Jericho and his men. In the early days of his youth, Jericho would have shot the man on sight, but he had a businessman's reputation to uphold, which was fading fast.

"Shave," Jericho repeated.

Thaddeus approached Johnny nervously and met Johnny's eyes. Johnny nodded to Thaddeus with an 'it's okay' pantomime. Thaddeus took his scissors and clipped Johnny's thick beard. Thaddeus brushed shave cream onto the short stubble on Johnny's face. As Thaddeus shaved, the faded tattoos on Johnny's face became known. Thaddeus finished, and his clean face under his former beard was revealed. His tattoos increased their colors as if they were brought back to life.

"You," Jericho said, grumbling. "I thought so."

"Yep. Still alive," Johnny stated.

Jericho moved his hand to the kerchief around Johnny's neck. Jericho pulled it down. It exposed a large, deep rope burn around Johnny's neck. He couldn't believe that the neck was scarred and not snapped.

"Damn…"

"Didn't finish the job."

"And now you're back… So, what do you want?'

"You have something that belongs to me. You all do."

"Well, whether it's revenge or whatever it is, you're not gettin' any of it."

"So, where does that leave us? Another hanging?"

"Oh, we're gonna hang ya. This time, we're gonna do it right," Jericho sneered. He turned to one of the henchmen. "Get the rope."

Two gang members pulled Johnny out of the barber chair and departed the shop. Jericho hadn't strung up someone in some time, but he hoped this would be the last—reputation be damned!

§

Jericho and his men forced a tied-up Johnny to walk down the main street like a shamed pariah. The townspeople provided their usual stares and gawks, similar to when he gunned down Jericho's men in the street.

"Get his horse," Jericho commanded. One of his men did what the boss instructed.

The townspeople came out of the various buildings with Cyrus and Jessy coming out of theirs. Jessy viewed Johnny's shaven face and realized Jericho knew what she knew. Cyrus also viewed Johnny's shaven face. His mouth gaped open in shock and surprise. He had seen this stranger before, and he had a name.

"One gun gets it done," he murmured. He was careful not to let Jericho and his men hear those cursed words.

"What are you going to do to him?" Jessy said.

"Since you two are so interested in helpin' him out, you can come and see. Maybe I'll let you join him." Jericho said. He gestured to some of his lackeys, who overpowered and abducted Cyrus and Jessy.

The men dragged them into the middle of the street. Jericho pulled his pistol from the holster and fired his gun in the air. His action startled the townspeople into silence. They knew he meant business as the gang's bullets still decorated the town.

"We have a situation here," Jericho bellowed. He pointed at Johnny with his gun. "This interloper has terrorized this town and has killed many of my men."

Jericho pointed at Cyrus and Jessy with an accusatory but theatrical flair. He wanted the townsfolk to know he meant business and that any of them were alive because he allowed them to be.

"And these two have aided and abetted this interloper," Jericho said. "Now, since this is a private matter, we will handle this interloper and his accomplices accordingly. There is no need to panic, and you are free to go about your business."

The townspeople stood frozen, unsure of what to do with themselves in the presence of Jericho's menace.

"Go on now," Jericho assured. "We'll handle this."

The townspeople slowly continued their business. Jericho turned and met Johnny's face, which mocked him with a frown drenched in melodrama.

"No audience?" Johnny said. He feigned disappointment and added a slight cock of his head to the right; all the while, he maintained a derisive pout. "Too bad. I thought we'd give 'em a show."

"Oh, you're gonna have a show all right," Jericho growled. "This one's gonna be your curtain call."

Jericho and his gang mounted their horses. The gang grabbed Jessy and Cyrus and mounted them on horses with a man on each side. Another brought Johnny's horse and mounted Johnny upon it. Jericho and his men escorted Johnny, Cyrus, and Jessy to the outskirts of town to a place that would seal their doom.

ELEVEN

ERICHO TOOK JOHNNY, JESSY, AND CYRUS TO A DESOLATE area far outside the town. An animal grazing area was staked out. Barbed wire was strung around it to keep the animals from escaping, but it was vacant. Nearby was a cottonwood tree. Like a conductor with his orchestra, Jericho stepped out and guided his aides to take Johnny to the tree and the other members to take Jessy and Cyrus to the side.

"Looks familiar," Johnny observed. "Tree's a little bigger than last time."

"Shut up," Jericho growled.

One of the men threw the rope over one of the large branches. Another accessory guided Johnny on his horse to the hanging tree.

"Take his gun," said one of the gang members toward the other member nearest to Johnny's horse.

"Never mind about that. We'll bury him with it," Jericho replied to the man as he winked at Johnny. "Don't say I never gave you nothin'."

The noose was placed around Johnny's neck. One of the men slapped the backside of Johnny's horse, and the Equus moved out from under Johnny. Johnny tried to breathe, but it became impossible. The rope pulled tight. Johnny went limp with his head pulled back as the noose continued to tighten, and his last hard breath was exhaled from his lungs as his life came to an end. Jericho turned to Johnny's horse and summoned one of his clan.

"Take care of his goddamn horse," Jericho growled.

The man advanced on Johnny's horse, took out his gun, and shot the horse at point-blank range. The horse shook his head as the bullet proved useless. The horse faced his would-be assassin. The shooter, in the heat of panic, shot at the horse repeatedly and emptied his pistol on the horse. There were no wounds, no blood, nothing. The beast reared up on its back hooves and knocked the man over. It stomped and trampled the thug to death. Upon the mangling of the shooter's body, Johnny's eyes snapped open. He craned his head forward toward his chest.

"Y'all have to do a better job than this."

Johnny's head rose off his chest. He smiled at Jericho and his men. The horde on the ground's faces fell. Cyrus and Jessy's mouths agape.

CRACK!

The sizeable hanging tree branch snapped off and fell to the ground. Johnny landed gracefully on his feet and removed the noose from his neck.

One man turned and ran toward him. Johnny grabbed the barbed wire off the fence and threw it at the lackey. It coiled around him and ripped him apart. Crimson viscera sprayed and pumped out of the man and into the grazing area.

Another accessory drew his gun. Johnny covered the heart tattoo on his bottom lip with his right thumb, drew his gun across his body with his left hand, and shot. The bullet pierced the man's heart, killing him. One of the men who was guarding Jessy stepped out in front of her, pulled out his gun, and aimed at Johnny. A shot rang out. The gang member looked at his gun in bewilderment. He hadn't fired it. His hand jerked up to his throat and pulled it away. His palm was covered in blood, and he fell to the ground, dead. Jessy held a small derringer pistol. Alonzo, behind Cyrus, turned to Jessy. She had the drop on him. Jessy pointed the derringer straight into Alonzo's face.

Johnny covered the club tattoo on his left cheek. One of the posts in the fence pulled itself out of the ground and hurled itself upon one of the men. The post rammed through his face. The man's skull shattered. It turned his face into a ground-up pulp of tissue and gore. Jericho's minions drew. Johnny used the five bullets left in his gun and mowed them all down, dead in their tracks.

Alonzo, still behind Cyrus, ran away from the two hostages. He took advantage of Johnny's mayhem. Jessy turned back and shot at him but missed as Alonzo went into a full sprint in a desperate escape from this carnage. Johnny covered the diamond tattoo with his right index finger on his right cheek. He turned sideways toward Alonzo and, with his left arm and hand extended at shoulder level, jutted out his four fingers and wiggled them around in his direction. Alonzo continued running, looking back with a puzzled look at Johnny. He tripped over a rock and fell into the sand. A den of diamondback rattlesnakes pounced upon Alonzo. They shook their rattles and struck him with their fangs. He screamed and pleaded in terror. The onslaught continued until the rattlesnakes' work was done. They left Alonzo's body a poisoned, bloody, misshapen mass.

Jericho pulled his gun and pointed it at Johnny. A *whoosh* of a knife came to an end as it sank deeply into Jericho's right wrist. Jericho screamed, dropped his gun, and looked in the direction of Cyrus. His belt displayed an empty knife sheath. In a seething rage, Jericho pulled out the knife from his wrist. He tried to reach for his gun on the ground, but the gun was shot at again and again, each time further away from his reach. He looked up and saw Johnny and his smoking gun. A grin formed upon Jericho's face. He clapped his hands in applause and put his hands up in feigned surrender.

"Looks like you're gonna get your revenge after all. I don't know what tricks you've been pulling, but they're the best I've ever seen. Congratulations!" Jericho mocked. Johnny stopped and froze where he stood.

"What are you waiting for?" Jericho bellowed. "Here's the chance to gun me down. There'll be others far worse than me, but go ahead!"

Johnny put his gun away. Jericho smiled a mile wide and continued to laugh. He knew this fool never had the guts to gun him down. He was weak — they all were.

"What's the matter?" crowed Jericho. "Lose your nerve?"

"I'm not the one," Johnny replied. He went into his shirt pocket and pulled a small, thin, brown whistle.

"What- what the hell is that?" Jericho mocked. He was unaware of what he had awakened. Johnny recalled where he received the strange object. He sat on the ground and opened the sack while Herrick and Olowin looked at him. The sack got turned over, and a skinny brown whistle was revealed in his hand. He channeled his dead friends.

"It's called a bone whistle. Made from the bone of an eagle," Herrick explained.

"It's been told that Crazy Horse used a similar whistle to lead his warriors into battle and frighten his enemies," Olowin added.

Johnny handled the whistle, remembering the day he'd received it. He grieved for all the ones that had fallen in this town. He gave a cold stare to Jericho, whose jocularity faded and was replaced with a look of bewilderment.

"Legend has it that it can…" Johnny's voice trailed off. He viewed Herrick and Olowin, still seated. They mouthed the words in unison, forcing their spirits through Johnny: "Summon spirits."

Johnny went to the mouthpiece of the bone whistle and blew into it. A loud, screeching sound emanated from the whistle like a wake of black vultures lauding over the remains of an unknown beast. He took the whistle from his lips. A louder response of hundreds of bone whistles came back. Jericho heard the whistles while Cyrus and Jessy cupped their ears. Johnny covered the spade tattoo with his right index finger between his nose and mouth.

Herrick and Olowin rose out of the ground on each side of Jericho. They both carried the same large metal axes from their act. Jericho turned to Herrick, who had a large, open wound on his bare chest. Jericho's mouth gaped open. He recalled in his rotten mind taking Herrick's axe. Herrick, who Jericho had some henchmen hold fast. He slammed Herrick's axe hard into Herrick's chest and pulled it out. Herrick's blood flowed out of his chest, and he fell face-first into the sand. Jericho's mind returned and saw the blood that dripped from Herrick's axe—Herrick's blood.

Jericho turned towards Olowin, whose face was beaten to the point of being unrecognizable. Still, Jericho observed that the top of Olowin's head was a circle of dried blood and was misshapen at the top. Jericho's mind flashed again. He saw himself beating Olowin with a large wooden post. Two men held Olowin, and he took a ferocious beating. Olowin's axe was lying next to him. Jericho dropped the wooden post and picked up the axe. He circled behind Olowin. The men held him from behind. Jericho stood behind him, put the axe on the top of Olowin's forehead, and started cutting his skin. He ruthlessly and viciously scalped Olowin. Jericho removed the scalp of Olowin and tossed it aside. Jericho raised the axe and struck hard upon Olowin's head.

Jericho's mind came back again to see Olowin's axe blade, covered in blood and gore. The spirit of these men came back for revenge.

Herrick and Olowin raised their axes and attacked Jericho from both sides. They slashed and hacked through Jericho's body. Jericho cried and hollered. His torso tore open, his face lacerated with cuts, and limbs severed from his body. Herrick and Olowin continued their assault; the sand opened up. Herrick, Olowin, and Jericho were pulled under the sand. They sank further into the ground. Herrick and Olowin welcomed this occurrence. They continued the hack and slash of Jericho. The sand swallowed them up.

When the retribution ended, Johnny picked up one of the dead men and slung him over the front of his saddle and onto the neck of his horse. He moved to another dead felon, picked him up, and slung the corpse over the back of the saddle. Cyrus and Jessy approached the horse. Unsure what to make of Johnny and if they were next.

"How in the world did you do all that, mister?" Cyrus asked.

Johnny slung another dead body over the back of the saddle.

"What's that?" Johnny replied. "Oh, just some tricks I learned along the way. I brought a few friends to help. Just got lucky."

"Never saw anything like that in my life," Jessy stated.

"Both of you had something to do with that, of course. Much obliged for the help."

"What are you going to do with the rest of 'em?" Cyrus inquired.

"Oh, I'll be back to get the rest. There's time. There's always time."

"Should bring you a nice haul with the bounty money and all. What happened to Jericho?"

"Let my friends have 'em."

"Dug a tunnel and pulled him under, eh?" Cyrus said.

"Somethin' like that." Johnny winked.

"Gonna cut you in for his reward money?"

"I have what I need," Johnny assuredly said. He climbed upon his horse. Jessy approached the side of Johnny's horse.

"When you're finished, you're coming back?"

"No."

"No?"

"There are more."

"More?"

"Many… more."

Johnny removed his hat, craned his head, and scratched his shorn, jet-black hair. A strong wind whipped up around him. It tousled his hair and revealed two small horns protruding from his scalp. The wind moved back and forth through Johnny's hair. Cyrus examined Johnny's hair. He tried to stifle his outburst—he couldn't.

"What the devil?" Cyrus yelled.

Johnny's face broke into a sly smile. "You never asked me what kind of god I was."

Cyrus and Jessy stood frozen, unsure of what to do.

"You've got nothin' to fear from me," assured Johnny. "The town doesn't either."

Jessy looked into Johnny's eyes. She remembered something. Her eyes moved to the tree where Johnny was 'hanged.' A vision of that day flashed into her mind. She tried to fight it off, but the power of the incident was too strong.

§

Caked in blood, Jessy walked through the dust-blown desert. A man was swinging by the neck from a tree. Jessy stopped and stared at the hanging figure from a distance.

§

The melee from the gang ceased. Angus Stillman, with his fabric tape, measured the bodies. He looked the same in the past as he did in the present. He finished measuring one body and then turned to measure another. His face wrinkled up like a dried prune. He only saw an outline of a body carved in the sand. Angus turned to one of his assistants and pointed at the outline. The assistant shook his head. Angus shrugged his shoulders and moved to the next dead body. The wind whipped up in the town, and the sand outline of the body blew away.

§

Jessy moved closer to the hanging figure. It was clad in the outfit that Johnny used to wear but was far less worn. She came to the terrifying realization it was indeed Johnny hanging from that tree. Jessy continued on, shocked by what she saw. She stopped short when she viewed from a distance a man who walked over to Johnny's dead horse. His outfit and face were completely covered in sand, obscuring his features. The man took his hands and gestured toward the horse like a conductor with a symphony built to a crescendo.

The horse awakened from its death slumber. It slowly raised its head and shook to life. The man repeated the gesture, and the horse slowly rose. The man took out a gun from his side pocket, walked over to the hanging tree, and shot the rope, severing it. Johnny's body fell to the ground. The man took out a knife, kneeled, and cut the noose off Johnny. Once this chore was completed, he turned and saw Jessy in the distance. A large gust of wind blew. It revealed the man's features. Jessy recognized him — Archer McCoy from the sideshow!

Archer still leaned towards Johnny. He rubbed his hands together and placed his hands upon Johnny's deceased body. A rumble of horses' hooves and gunshots was heard closer and closer toward Jessy, Johnny, and Archer. Jessy turned toward the sound and became Jessy from twelve years ago. Jessy ran away from the sound. Archer and the body of Johnny disappeared. They left the severed rope on the tree that swayed back and forth in the wind.

§

Jessy stared at Johnny on his horse. She extracted herself from her visions courtesy of some supernatural ability that either he or she possessed. He smiled at her as he placed his hat back on his head. Jessy wanted to say something to him, but Cyrus beat her to it.

"You ain't after that kind of bounty," Cyrus whispered.

Johnny tipped his hat to Cyrus and Jessy. He made a coaxing noise between his teeth. The horse moved toward the trail. It left Jessy and Cyrus still as statues. Johnny, his horse, and the two dead bodies rode out onto the trail out of the down.

Jessy broke from her idle appearance and ran towards Johnny to talk with him again. She stopped when she realized that Johnny and his horse were far away in the distance. She wanted to tell him about her vision and the man who committed his resurrection. *Was he indeed a demon? Did something in his eyes reveal this secret only to me, or did he know it was Archer all along?* Jessy may never know the answer or if the sun's heat made her delirious. She watched as Johnny became smaller in the distance. Jessy wanted to dismiss this daydream, but her will couldn't allow it. Her dream was real. It had to be! Jessy would tell Johnny when he returned for the rest—if he ever returned.

Johnny eyed Old Glory whipping in the wind, caught on sagebrush. Freed from the pole that held it, its wind dance interrupted. A bemused smile came upon his face, knowing that this Star-Spangled Banner would become obsolete when one star was added. Still, other territories and states would be vying for a white star in that field of marine blue. The lawful by any means to make it happen, and the lawless doing their damnest to prevent it. This meant more people had something of his that he must claim. The good and bad of this job. The good: exact justice upon the scourge of the land. The bad: kill without prejudice. This was too black and white for him. There were far too many shades of grey to slay. Upon his restoration of life, he was instructed to feed a furnace with the black souls of these dead men to keep the flames of hell a-burnin'. The horse would guide him to where the sand departed. A massive black cast iron furnace rose from the depths. Its features were similar to an oversized wood-burning stove fit for an ogre. The kind of ogre that resided in the stories his mother read him as a child before bedtime. Its door flew open, and cascades of flames licked the insides of its giant maw. Johnny would throw in their remains. The maw slammed shut, and the bodies were voraciously devoured in mere minutes — the furnace was insatiable!

He never knew who brought him back from the hanging. It was apparent why fate had chosen him, and the prospects of immortality looked him in the eye. No mortal being nor anything on this earth could kill him. Death wasn't in the cards. He could only hope some mystical force would take him to the journey's end. Until then, the furnace and its fire must be fed — with as many souls he could kill and carry.

Johnny sighed and snapped the reins out of habit, as the horse didn't need to be coaxed to guide him to the next venture. They rode toward the red sun stretching across the sky. It had begun descending the horizon, creating another sundown in Prosperity.

§

A plateau rose above the trail with a horse that stood silently upon it. The upland looked down on the trail as Johnny and his horse continued towards the horizon. A boot and a pant leg in a stirrup indicated someone was on this horse. The dusk came upon the rocks; it revealed Archer McCoy. He wore the same outfit he had performed in some twelve years ago: shabby and worn from age and neglect. His head was exposed. It revealed the same small horns that Johnny had, but they were much more pronounced with his continually thinning hair. A small, circular scar was visible in the middle of his forehead as he held his top hat in his right hand.

Archer put his top hat on his head. He reached into his pocket with his right hand and pulled something out with a closed fist. He opened his fist, placed a silver coin on his thumb, and flipped it up in the air. He caught it with his left hand. He repeated this action, flipped another silver coin with his right hand, and then caught it with his left. Archer grinned and opened his mouth. His bluish gums contrasted with tobacco-stained teeth. He emitted a hearty laugh that shook through his skeletal frame. He would meet up with Johnny one day. If not in this world, then the next one.

THE END

ACKNOWLEDGMENTS

I want to acknowledge the following people for making this book happen:

—Adrian Medina at Fabled Beast Designs for his tremendous feedback on the story, invaluable suggestions, fantastic cover art, and expert book formatting. A man of many trades.

—Candace Nola and her staff at 360 Publishing. Your insights and efforts to improve my writing have been invaluable. I am grateful for all of the help.

—Lisa Branum for her patience and encouragement for all the times I've wanted to quit on this story and the writing profession for good. You've always been there and have had my back for more times than I deserved. I love you.

ABOUT THE AUTHOR

Paul Grammatico resides in the San Francisco Bay Area. *Six Bullets at Sundown* is his fourth book and fifth published story. Paul is an avid fan of cult movies and books of various genres. He is working on a short story collection, a sports novel, and a giallo.

When he isn't reading, writing, or being a podcast guest on Movies from Hell, he watches serial TV shows with his significant other, Lisa, and their four cats.

Paul can be found on the following platforms:

Twitter (X): @paul_grammatico

Instagram: @paulgrammatico

Facebook: https://www.facebook.com/paulgramm66

TikTok:https://www.tiktok.com/@horror.writer. pg?lang=en

BOOKS BY THE AUTHOR

After their Grandmother's death, Alexis and her siblings arrive at her house to clean and tidy up the vast, two-story French Colonial. During their purging and rearranging, Dante, their brother, ignores his cleaning duties and provides a sizeable antique jar he discovers filled with various skeleton keys. He convinces his sisters and wife to select and explore the house to find which keys open any of the doors within the hallways of the neglected mansion. As each family member selects a key, it opens doors to their terrifying memories from which there is no escape.

Now on Amazon and www.ejectpress.com!

Five hunters head up to Northern Michigan in the dead of winter during deer hunting season in a desolate place called Starvation Lake. When a horrifying accident occurs, leaving an elderly woman fatally wounded with no help in sight and then covering up their crime in the deep snow. In its aftermath, the hunters face numerous perils in the surrounding pristine woods, which begin to turn on them. As the hunters' lives are in jeopardy, they realize that the dead woman's words are not a plea but a curse.

Now on Amazon and www.ejectpress.com!

Insects of the Damned

Many strange things happen in a small town, but for local law enforcement and an eccentric scientist, this was more than they bargained for in their town of Mintonka, Minnesota. An insect invasion in a small farming town cuts a swath of gruesome terror. A group of locals join forces to locate the cause of how these insects are alive, how their carnivorous tendencies came about, and what can be done to destroy them.

Now on Amazon!